WRITING TALKS

WRITING PROGRAM DIRECTOR LINGUIST

WRITING TALKS

VIEWS ON TEACHING WRITING FROM ACROSS THE PROFESSIONS

Edited by

Muffy E. A. Siegel

and

Toby Olson

Temple University

SOCIAL WORKER

INTERNATIONAL BANKER

DEPARTMENT CHAIRMAN EPA OFFICIAL

POET

PHILOSOPHER

PSYCHOLOGIST

ENGLISH

BOYNTON/COOK PUBLISHERS, INC.
UPPER MONTCLAIR, NEW JERSEY 07043

Library of Congress Cataloging in Publication Data

Writing talks.

"Poet, philosopher, social worker, psychologist, writing program director, linguist, international banker, Environmental Protection Agency official, English Department chairman."
  1. English language—Rhetoric—Study and Teaching—Addresses, essays, lectures.   I. Siegel, Muffy E. A., 1950-   . II. Olson, Toby.
PE1404.W735 1983   808'.042   83-11891
ISBN 0-86709-077-4

Copyright © 1983 by Boynton/Cook Publishers, Inc. All rights reserved. No part of this book may be used or reproduced in any manner without written permission except in the case of brief quotations embodied in critical articles and reviews.

For information address Boynton/Cook Publishers, Inc.
P.O. Box 860, Upper Montclair, New Jersey 07043

ISBN: 0-86709-077-4

Printed in the United States of America

83 84 85 86   10 9 8 7 6 5 4 3 2 1

This book is for
George Deaux

This book is published with the aid of a grant from the Fund for the Improvement of Postsecondary Education.

The editors wish to thank Alice Ginsberg for her invaluable editorial aid in preparing the manuscript for publication.

Preface

Most of the following essays were initially presented as papers in a series of seminars on student writing that was supported, in part, by a grant from the Fund for the Improvement of Postsecondary Education. The seminars were part of a larger grant program that was designed to train members of departments other than English to teach college composition courses and, at the same time, to add to the increasing body of knowledge about the teaching of composition. The activities associated with the retraining grant provided an environment in which scholars with backgrounds quite different from those of traditional English teachers were turning their attention to the problems of teaching composition. During the seminars upon which this book is based, experts in even more diverse fields were invited to analyze and propose solutions to appropriate problems in the teaching of writing. It became clear that there is a fortunate side to the current prevalence of writing difficulties. Not only faculty from departments other than English, but also people in business, industry, and the other professions are concerning themselves with the problems of teaching writing, and often their special expertise is extremely helpful for understanding and solving some of these problems. This text, then, brings together studies of four major problems in the teaching of writing.

Contents

Preface

Introduction

Part I REVISION   1

  1. Teaching Writing Where It Happens: An Approach to the
     Revision Process *Toby Olson*   3
  2. Revision: Another Look *Joe Fitschen*   14

Part II THE INDIVIDUAL CONFERENCE   29

  3. The Individual Conference: The Psychological Gap   31
     Grace Ganter
  4. Some Psychological Implications of Student-Teacher
     Conferences *Linda Hillman*   40
  5. Student Worlds in Student Conferences *Stephen Zelnick* 47

Part III THE TEACHING OF GRAMMAR   59

  6. Teaching Grammar: Some Linguistic Predictions
     Justine T. Stillings and Muffy E. A. Siegel   61
  7. Discourse Organization in Speech and Writing
     Donald Hindle   71
  8. Syntactic Interference from the Spoken Language in the
     Prose of Unskilled Writers *Anthony S. Kroch*   87

Part IV AUDIENCE   103

  9. On Writing in the Real World *Harold van B. Cleveland* 105
10. Writing for the Human Services *Miriam Meltzer Olson*   112
11. Teaching Writers at a Government Agency *John R. Adams*   125
12. Models for Writing *Richard C. Newton*   135

Introduction

It may be pleasant to imagine a time when the teaching of writing was thought of as aimed toward the refinement of certain products that students had the skills to produce. In such days, student essays could be fruitfully examined and talked about as close to finished works, and issues that were familiar and congenial to the expertise of literary scholars and critics—the traditional teachers of writing—were the ones composition courses comfortably dealt with.

Whether or not such days ever existed, it's clear that student essays that lend themselves to such examinations are rare today, and teachers of high school writing and beginning college composition courses now find themselves confronted with pre-product issues, issues that have more to do with the process that goes into the making of adequate essays than the analysis of them. This shift to an examination of process rather than product, in addition to informing much of contemporary composition theory and research, broadens the scope of expertise that is relevant to the teaching of writing. The professional writer, for example, though he may have little to say about the finished work, knows perhaps better than anyone else what happens to the writer and his writing during the making of it. In addition, if the writing process and the process of learning to write are seen from an even broader point of view, many other areas of expertise are found to be appropriate to solving the problems that arise. Philosophers, psychologists, social workers, linguists, even bankers and government officials are experts on various aspects of what goes on with a writer and with his writing, aspects which may escape the attention of English teachers with traditional, product oriented backgrounds.

This book is an attempt to bring the expertise from fields not usually associated with the composition classroom to some problems in the teaching of writing. Since the current crisis in writing ability has necessitated teaching writing not only across the curriculum but also in business and industry, we have been able to gather essays from those who have given considerable thought to writing problems and have set out, in their various disciplines and work places, to solve them. This book does not attempt to address itself to every writing problem. Rather, it focuses discussion upon four major areas of concern: Revision, the Individual Conference, Grammar, and Audience.

Revision

To write well, a person must at least have a desire to do so and an intention to express something. However, though they may have the desire—whether to gain good grades or for higher motives—students often come to composition classes either without intentions or with ones that are vague and ill-formed. Often, this is as it should be, for much good writing emerges from the process in which it is made, and firm, detailed intentions that are formulated prior to actual writing can be a hindrance to discovery.

One of the difficult tasks of the writing teacher is to help student writers see that they have something to write about, to help them find ways to form and reform their intentions, both before and as they write. One way to this end is through the use of "tools" that students can use to help them make choices and effect change as they write. Seen in this way, revision is part of the activity of writing itself and not a matter of proofreading for errors in an ostensibly finished product.

A central difficulty in teaching revision is that the process of each writer is unique, and to impose a common set of tools for revision on student writers may well impede the individual writer in finding his or her own special writing procedures. The first two essays in this collection, one by a poet, the other by a philosopher, address the issue of revision in both theoretical and practical ways. Though they disagree on some points, they both see revision as a personal and idiosyncratic process that at the same time contains elements that can be taught to students so that they can form and understand their own revision procedures and thereby produce better writing.

The Individual Conference

One of the most frustrating facts about teaching students to become writers is that they tend to experience their difficulties with writing in very personal ways. This is in part because they are aware of their failure to master principles of good writing in almost every college course they attend and, even more seriously, they experience their lacks as writers as lacks in self. Where teachers of composition most profoundly come into contact with these perceived lacks is the individual conference. Indeed, in many universities, it is *only* the teacher of composition who has the opportunity to come into extensive contact with first-year students in conference. The individual conference, then becomes the circumstance in which the teacher must often confront difficulties that, while focused in writing, go well beyond it. The second group of essays—by a psychologist, a social worker, and a writing program director—examine the dynamics of the individual conference as a circumstance in which two people come together in a task-oriented setting. Essays 3 and 4 focus on psychological problems which may make it difficult for students to allow themselves to be helped in conferences and on ways that teachers can attempt to avoid the worst effects of these problems. Essay 5 explores ways that teachers can use knowledge of the socioeconomic forces that have shaped their students both to circumvent psychological problems and to teach effective writing in conferences.

The Teaching of Grammar

To many English teachers, the application of theoretical linguistics to the problems of teaching composition will not seem new. Many ideas which passed as findings of Noam Chomsky and other transformational-generative grammarians were presented to teachers of writing in the sixties. Unfortunately, these first implications of linguistics for teaching writing were often drawn by those not highly trained in linguistic theory. The implications of the new work in linguistics were often taken to be either that there was no need to teach grammar at all since everyone already had a perfectly good grammar, or that it would be nearly trivial to teach grammar since writing teachers would simply have to hand students the complete and explicit formulation of all the rules of standard English that linguists would soon come up with.

Neither of these positions is correct, and neither of them follows from an understanding of work in generative-transformational grammar. Naturally, although each student can be said to speak his own dialect perfectly, it will be necessary for him to learn the grammar of standard written English if he is to make his way in American society at large. Yet the work of theoretical linguistics will not help us teach students grammar directly; the "rules" that linguists write are part of a descriptive theoretical construct to account for spoken English; they are not instructions for how to write.

So the problem remains. Students must learn to use the grammar and organization of standard written English, a language they may be only minimally familiar with, yet our traditional methods of teaching grammar by means of exercises based on prescriptive rules formulated in the traditional way have little effect on the grammar students use in their writing. However, the linguists represented in this book, all working theoretical linguists with a special interest in the teaching of writing, believe that we can improve writing instruction if we examine more carefully the various types of and reasons for student deviation from standard written English. The first paper in this section, essay 6, shows that such research has very clear implications for how best to formulate grammatical rules for writing and to sequence grammar teaching. Essays 7 and 8 report on research indicating that beginning writers suffer as much from following in their writing certain constraints appropriate to speech as they do from failing to follow special rules for writing, a finding with important implications for teaching.

Audience

Composition teachers know that before students can become more than minimally competent in writing they must arrive at some understanding of the role of an imagined audience. A student who tries to write with *no* audience in mind is likely to feel paralyzed; humans do not ordinarily produce language with no communicative purpose. Moreover, careful consideration of the needs of a particular audience will lead students to shape their essays' tone, vocabulary and even structure in ways characteristic of good writing.

For most composition teachers, audience issues are revealed through models, those usually found in the readers that play such a large part in most composition courses. But the essays in these readers are often ineffective as teaching tools. When the essays are very good, they are often too sophisticated for student readers, too distant from their verbal experience to be understandable models; when they are understandable, they are often superficial and slight. In addition, with most essays in these readers, the instructor must arrive at judgments about the specifics of their intended audience from the text itself, and since most good essays do not talk about their intended audience, these judgments must be both questionable and superficial.

Essays 9 through 12, the last group in this book, come from people who represent the actual audiences for student writing, present and future. The first three—from banking, the human services, and a government agency—discuss the audience issue from various practical points of view, including those of ethics, politics, and effective business practices. The last, from a college English department chairman, addresses the issue of models for good writing in a general way, confronting directly the political implications of the use of models in teaching.

All the essays in this book are based on the premise that students become good writers through the acquisition of a cluster of learnable skills, outlooks, and habits of thought. The teacher's responsibility is to formulate and analyze these and to help students adopt them. To this end, some of the essays here concentrate on ways to define and introduce rules and tools that students can really use in writing (essays 1 and 6), while others describe in detail the types of outlook necessary for writing for various purposes (essays 9, 10, and 11). Yet, it must be recognized that the "new ways" involved in becoming a good writer are not easy for students to adopt and that these new ways sometimes affect more than writing. At the least, writing well involves abandoning many language constraints that have guided students' previous language behavior (essays 7 and 8). For many students, too, becoming a good writer requires giving up some psychological coping mechanisms that have served them all their lives (essays 3, 4, and 5). Indeed, learning to write well entails becoming, to some degree, a different kind of person (essays 2 and 12). Such changes are, of course, what we hope for in education. The essays in this book all attempt to identify what students need to change in themselves to become writers so that we can acknowledge and build on what there is no need to change.

WRITING TALKS

PART I

Revision

1

Teaching Writing Where It Happens:

An Approach to the Revision Process

TOBY OLSON

Toby Olson has published numerous books of poetry and two novels, the most recent of which, Seaview (New Directions), *received the PEN/Faulkner award for the most distinguished work of fiction by an American in 1982. In addition to conducting writing workshops throughout the country, he has taught both creative writing and composition courses at The Aspen Writers' Workshop, Long Island University, The New School for Social Research, and Temple University, where he is currently Associate Professor of English.*

The context in which a practicing poet comes together with a group of beginners with expectations is similar, in a certain way, to the context in which a teacher of English composition arranges for the possibility of learning in his or her class. Regardless of methods and materials used, in both cases the subject matter of the course is the students' writing, and that writing starts and finishes from nothing outside the students' individual bodies. In an extreme but not atypical case, a student can have a good understanding of rhetorical or poetic modes, a reasonable mastery of grammar and argumentative principle (even an appreciation of successful models) and still not be able to write well; somehow, the translation of this external material into forms that can be used in the student's own particular writing process has not been made. A teacher can push and manipulate writing, can make suggestions about it, can assign the direction of it. But only the students can make it; in this sense it is always creative writing. It isn't Stevens, of course, though it's easy to see the beginning poet aspire to such skill. It isn't Edward Dahlberg either, though it may give the teaching of English composition its proper status to point out that the process students engage in is not different from his.

What I will talk about here is what I am going to call "the activity of revision," and a few things need to be said by way of clarification before I begin. First of all, when I use the word "process" I'm not referring to what is usually called the "creative process." I'm not sure I know exactly what creativity is, and I certainly don't know what teaching creativity would mean.

My concern is not with psychological states, mental events, or any generalizations about what happens in the minds of writers when they write. The kernel of what I want to argue is that it's possible to formulate certain "tools" that students can use in specific helpful ways while they are revising any kind of writing they might engage in. My assumption is that growth in mastery in the activity of revision is a necessary condition for good writing of any kind.

Though I don't wish to slight the importance of prewriting exercises and other formalized kinds of preparations that may be taught to students as aids to getting underway with their writing, I will not be talking about such preparations at all. It is the rare student who comes to me with problems that have to do with getting started. The question most often is, "Now that I've written this stuff, how do I make it right?" For me, the answer to that question lies in an examination of revision, and when I speak of revision as an "activity" I mean to speak of it as a group of conscious acts that writers make and can, as beginning writers, be taught to make more successfully.

I'm going to begin by outlining some ways in which I go about teaching courses in poetry writing. The course model that follows that discussion is an attempt to point out how these ways might be applied in courses in English composition.

Teaching a poetry workshop

In the first meeting of a poetry workshop class, it's my practice to present the students with a context in which meaningful discussion of their poetry can best take place. The context is both specific and extreme, and its purpose is in part to focus, and at the same time leave room for, the more impressionistic (often more important) discussions that are necessary to a class of this kind. This context can best be described in reference to three connected areas of concern: intention, value judgment, and audience.

Intention

All discussions of student poems (both in class and in conference) focus on the relationship between the poet's intentions and the poem he or she has written and not on the poem itself, and a poem is judged to be finished or unfinished insofar as its effects (as articulated by the poet, the class, and the instructor) conform to the effects the poet had intended. Even if, for example, the class is unanimous in its judgment that a poem is successful in very specific ways, unless these ways are consistent with the poet's intentions the poem is not considered a successful (or finished) one.

In this context, intention is defined as *the grounds on which a writer makes decisions for or against change in the activity of revision.* This operational definition of intention marks the distinction between revision and writing; when it applies, the activity in which it applies is called revision. In the case in which a poet writes a complete poem, usually at one sitting, without making any conscious decisions at the time, it is assumed that he or she will "read the poem over" at least once; in this reading the activity of revision will take place.

The above definition of intention is, of course, a more limited one than the usual. It excludes all intentional prewriting choices, most initial choices about subject matter, and most "secondary" intentions, such as those having to do with impressing readers or gaining good grades. It also excludes revision choices made on the grounds of intuition, visions, automatic writing, etc.; in short, it excludes any choice that is self-justifying. It is not that these grounds for choice are wrong; indeed, they may be *just* the ones that separate the finest writers from the majority. But the ways of choosing that such grounds generate cannot be taught, and the above definition of intention is designed to focus on areas in which teaching can take place.

The paradigm for a finished poem, then, is one about which the poet can fully articulate how the poem fulfills his or her intention. To paraphrase Louis Zukofsky (*A Test of Poetry* (New York: C. Z. Publications, 1980), p. 58): if one word in a poem can be changed and that change does not affect the poem, the poem is not finished. Stated another way, there can be nothing arbitrary about a finished poem, and the only way a poet can know this is through a total understanding of what the poem does. In practice, of course, this full understanding is never achieved. It is nevertheless aimed for, and it is in the struggle to achieve it, if often to find—through work—that a line, an image, or a word is finally unjustifiable yet correct, that learning takes place, that the poem gets made.

Value judgments

All poems discussed in the workshop are defined as being unfinished, and the purpose of the discussions and conferences is to help poets finish them. Judgments about the quality of subject matter or sentiment are seen as being beyond the purview of the workshop. In the workshop context, poems are never good or bad; they are either finished or unfinished. Value judgments of the kind intended to rank poems in terms of some particular set of standards of quality are seen as being part of the realm of literary criticism, an activity that takes place only after poems have left the workshop context, and the poets no longer have any control over them.

At the expense of getting ahead of myself, it's necessary to speak a little about grading here. In a poetry workshop class, it's not difficult to justify student effort as a ground for grading, but grading students in a composition course is a different matter, one that might seem especially problematic if the course is thought of as a workshop: a setting in which mastery of *how* a task is done is more important than the product itself. If the emphasis is on process, how can one justify grading students on product? My answer to this lies in again noting that what I am outlining here is a pragmatic model designed to focus work and not an exclusionary philosophy of composition.

In poetry workshops, students often come to me in conference wanting to know if their work is "any good." They ask the class this question at times as well; they ask us to be critics. And of course we answer them, as gently and responsibly as we can. In composition courses, at most places, it is clear from the beginning that students will finally be judged on the writing products they produce, and part of the task of the instructor is to translate articulated standards into goals that students can understand and pursue. I believe that mastery in revision is a necessary, but not always sufficient, condition for "good" writing, and I suggest the model that I am outlining here as a way of aiding students in mastering that process. In composition courses, through the use of models of good writing and clearly articulating course standards, grade goals can be set, progress toward them can be noted, and there need be nothing contradictory between doing that and applying the model I am outlining. After all, a primary goal of all students in composition courses must be, for whatever reason, to write well. It can hardly be to write poorly! And it is part of the composition teacher's task to present clearly what writing well means, what the course measure of good writing is. I think that often too much is made of the issue of process versus product in relation to grades, and that the real issue lies with the difficulty of articulating standards for good writing and not with the supposed contradiction. That's another matter, however, and it won't be dealt with here.

Audience

Since all the poems discussed in the poetry workshop class are considered to be unfinished, the class itself is seen as a kind of testing ground for the poem under consideration. In practice, this means that the class will usually spend some time acting as if the poem is a finished piece that they are reading in a book or magazine; the poet will remain silent for a while; the class will give the poet some sense of what has been accomplished relative to intentions. In the workshop context, the poet's desire to communicate his or her realized intentions in the specific poem is assumed. If the poet wishes to communicate nothing either through idea or feeling, there is no reason for discussing the poem in class.

The context described above is presented to the students as a model circumstance in which meaningful discussion of their poetry in class and in conference can take place. In practice, a variety of materials and teaching techniques is used in the course. Guest writers visit the class and talk about their work; the work of established poets whose concerns seem similar to the students' is considered; open and freewheeling discussions of issues arising from student poems often take place; value judgments about content are sometimes made; various poetic forms and structures are examined. However, the model controls in the sense that discussion of students' work always returns to what the context suggests is the central issue: the relationship between the students' intentions and their poems.

The situation in which the students must finally confront the issue of intention is revision. In the beginning of the semester, two things are assumed about revision. First, it is acknowledged that in the process of revising, events (intuitions, etc.) take place that are usually associated with the creative process. It is further acknowledged that the creative process may well be distinctly different for each student and that it isn't the intention of the workshop to make generalizations about it. Second, given the workshop definition of intention (*the grounds on which a writer makes decisions for or against change in the activity of revision*), revision is studied as the place where poems are made only insofar as intention can be talked about as grounds for change toward the refinement and ultimate finishing of the specific poem in question. Grounds, then, must yield to articulation: "I made this change because I wanted to accomplish this." Statements such as, "I made this change because it felt right" or "I made this change because I had a vision" are respected and accepted, but it is pointed out that such grounds for change cannot yield to alteration through argument, and while they may be fruitfully talked about in the workshop, they cannot be learned or taught in specific ways. Whatever such grounds proceed from (and they may proceed precisely from circumstances that make the best writers good), they are seen as being outside the teaching situation that the workshop model assumes.

In specific instances, revision problems usually take one of two forms. Either the poets are unclear about their intentions and are, therefore, unable to consider meaningful change, or the poets, while clear about their intentions, don't quite know how to go about making changes to fulfill them. One of the major tasks of the workshop is to provide the student poets with a group of tools they can use in the activity of revision to resolve difficulties with formulating and realizing intentions.

Tools

In the first session of the workshop, I suggest that students begin a list of specific devices they can use to look at poems or parts of poems while they are revising them. These devices may arise in class discussion, may be very limited or very comprehensive, may be obviously mechanical or even rather impressionistic. They may be suggested by something that a fellow student says, may arise in the activity of revision itself, or may be mentioned directly by me. I ask the students to think of these devices as tools, and I designate a tool as any device that can be clearly defined and used to resolve difficulties in the activity of revision. I suggest that the more tools students have at their disposal, the more ways they will have for looking into the complexities of their poems.

The tape recorder is a mechanism that is usually used in the workshop as a tool in a number of ways. Students often find that reading their poems into a tape recorder and then listening to them can help them define and/or resolve difficulties with form, voice, rhythm, syntax, etc. Thinking of a poem as having the underpinning of its force in its nouns and verbs is a tool that can help with loss of image power, too much density, over qualification, slowness, etc. (Often, counting the number of words that qualify certain nouns and verbs is helpful.) Asking the students to return to the "scene" of the poem and look again at the things they are attempting to present is a valuable tool as well. Listing the possible associations that a reader might have to a certain important word or image in a poem has also proved a useful device.

These are but a brief sampling of possible tools. I have made no attempt to categorize them, say, in terms of the defining or realizing of intention, for two reasons. First, the distinction between defining and realizing intentions is a convenience only. Often the two happen at the same time; what actually goes on in a particular student's revision process is far more complex and subtle than my language about revision suggests. Second, tools are valuable *only* in a pragmatic way, and that value comes only as students adjust tools to meet their own, often idiosyncratic ends; that is, tools have meaning and value only as students make them their own.

As the poetry workshop semester progresses, the number of tools increases. As students become more comfortable in using them, tools are redefined, expanded in use, rejected, incorporated into the specific activity of revision of specific students. By the end of the semester, in most successful cases, tools have become an integral part of the process of revision in individual ways. As tools (and not rules) they tend to be used in an unthreatening way; students don't report that tools do violence to or tamper with what they might call creativity. Indeed, the opposite seems to be true: tools are usually seen as instruments of power, ones that add force and complexity to the growth of the process of revision that students are developing. The central thing that students report about the use of tools is that they help them become increasingly self-sufficient in their writing.

Since the discipline of poets by its very nature has to do with writing poetry rather than studying the product produced by them, it's no wonder that the revision process emerges as a central consideration in poetry writing classes. Since for me *all* writing, when it comes to revision, is creative writing, over time I have begun to introduce these revision ideas into courses in English composition as well as poetry workshop classes. What follows is an example of how these ideas might be integrated into a college writing curriculum. (I suspect that they would be effective in high school writing classes as well.) Though this course model argues that it's a good thing to teach writing of all kinds in a composition course, the ideas it contains could as well be applied in a course limited to prose non-fiction. After I have presented the following course outline, I'll have a few final things to say about revision.

A Composition Course: "The Creative Activity of Writing"

Level: Though the course is conceived as an introduction to writing, its methods are also applicable in remedial and advanced writing courses.

Purpose: The purpose of this course is to help students understand (and control) revision, to provide them with a group of tools that they can use to this end, and to help them formulate and fulfill their intentions so that they can produce finished pieces of writing.

Assumptions:

A. No important distinction exists between the process involved in producing what is usually called Creative Writing and that involved in producing what is usually called English Composition.
B. The number of pieces students write has nothing to do, in itself, with whether or not they learn to write well.
C. The activity in which students learn to write is the activity of revision.
D. Meaningful revision (change or the consideration of change) can only take place in light of articulated intentions on the writer's part.
E. Revision tools can be clearly defined and taught.

Note: It may be that the assumption that revision is a conscious act isn't always true. Intuitive (or non-rational) decisions may play an essential role in the writing process that differs from writer to writer. This, however, is irrelevant in the sense that intuition cannot be taught. Tools for revision *can* be taught, and it's possible that in the teaching of a more complex and sophisticated revision process, more complex and sophisticated intuitions will occur.

Structure: The course consists of (1) inclass discussion of student writing, (2) inclass discussion of the revision process, (3) individual conferences with the instructor, and (4) presentation of tools for revision.

  A. Inclass discussion of student witing:
    1. Students write a variety of pieces (poems, stories, essays, etc.).
    2. All pieces of writing discussed in class are defined as being unfinished; this means that either the writer of a particular piece hasn't fulfilled his or her intentions or isn't clear about what the intentions are.
    3. The emphasis of the discussions is on helping writers finish the pieces they have submitted for class consideration.
      a. All writing that students present to either the class or the instructor (since it is by definition unfinished) is revised. Revision continues until the piece is finished or, by joint decision of the student and the instructor, abandoned.
      b. All students are expected to be constantly involved in the process of revision; that is, they are constantly working on their writing. There is no definite number of pieces to be written in the course. Each writer works at his or her own pace.

B. Inclass discussion of the revision process:
   1. The students are asked to share the specific ways in which they go about revising their work. They are asked to share methods and techniques that they have found useful as well as difficulties that they are trying to overcome.
   2. A major purpose for inclass discussion of the revision process is to make revision less mysterious.
C. Individual conferences with the instructor:
   1. The focus of the conferences is on revision of the students' writing.
   2. The conference is also, and most importantly, a chance for students to discuss their progress in relation to course standards.
D. The presentation of tools for revision:
   1. Throughout the semester, a good deal of time is spent in defining and presenting tools for revision.
   2. Students may invent their own tools, and these are given equal weight with those formulated by the instructor.

Tools: The assumption is made that every conceivable "error" an instructor may find in a piece of student writing can be related to revision as a process in which the student is trying to formulate and fulfill his or her intentions, thereby creating the finished piece.

Note: It may seem difficult to argue that simple grammatical and punctuation errors stand in the way of fulfilling intentions, yet traditional arguments for correcting such errors are not far from that. The point is often made that punctuation errors (and grammatical slips) are seen as flaws by the sophisticated reader and that they undercut the conviction of the writing. When the goal is to produce "finished" pieces, it becomes clear that pieces cannot be finished until such flaws are corrected. It's also easy to see how such flaws stand in the way of fulfilling specific intentions. When, for example, a misplaced comma appears in an otherwise well-crafted piece, the comma error will limit the success of the content just because it's there. All this, of course, includes assumptions about audience. Indeed, the context that I have been talking about throughout depends upon communication between writer and audience for its existence. There's much to be said (much that *is* said) these days about just what "audience" means and what it is. In this course, however, the audience is not viewed as "fictional," "ideal," or in any other way but real. The audience is the actual class and instructor involved.

A. Tools are treated pragmatically:
   1. For the most part, there's nothing unfamiliar about what is being suggested here as tools. A tool is any technique that can be clearly defined (by student or instructor) and applied in the process of revision. Only when a tool is clearly defined and applied can a student know whether or not the tool works in a given revision situation.

2. The more tools students have at their disposal the better able they will be to revise successfully and create finished pieces of writing.
B. A list of tools (five examples):
   1. The statement of purpose:
      a. When this tool is clearly defined, students may apply it at various stages of revision; it may help them judge development of argument, relevance of material, etc.
      b. The statement of purpose may be used to clarify the writer's intentions early in the revision process.
   2. The topic sentence:
      a. If students discover that paragraph structure is a problem, they may find use for this tool in revising specific paragraphs.
      b. The topic sentence may also be used to isolate and understand the nature of transition, digression, etc.
   3. Reading the piece into a tape recorder:
      a. Students may find this a useful tool in making judgments about awkwardness in style, sentence structure, authenticity of voice, etc.
      b. The tape recorder may be used in class discussions; fellow writers may be of help in pointing out difficulties that its use reveals.
   4. Reading for punctuation:
      a. If students find the comma to be a problem, they may discover that reading the paper *only* in search of that specific difficulty will be fruitful.
      b. The principle behind this tool may have application in the use of tools in general.
   5. Location:
      a. Thinking of the progress of a piece of writing as a movement of the reader from place to place may aid the student in resolving issues of tense, transition, argument (or image) progressions, etc.
      b. The location tool is related to "point of view."

Note: This list of tools seems to contain none specifically related to what is usually called Creative Writing. It's easy to see, however, how the tape recorder and location tools can be applied to story and poem contexts. A list of Creative Writing tools could be provided, but the important point is that *anything that can be clearly defined and used in revision is a tool.* If the topic sentence tool works when applied to an Imagist poem, then it's a good tool in that context.

The Writing:

A. The course assumes that the place in which students must handle the difficulties of writing is the activity of revision; it attempts to address that process directly.

B. So that students may be allowed to confront difficulties with the formulation of intentions, all writing assignments for the course are presented to them as general assignments that they will be forced to limit and define in their own terms.

Two notes on researching the course:

A. A Revision Journal may be used as a research instrument. Patterns of revision difficulties and useful tools may be extracted from class journals as a beginning in building some understanding of the nature of the revision process of the population that the class represents.

B. The course does not attempt to teach students how to write impromptu themes. It would seem that the rather methodical process of revision would be contradictory to it. If, however, learning about revision is (as the course assumes) learning about the basic process of writing, the effects of that learning may be felt in all kinds of writing. To test this, the course could begin and end with an impromptu essay. These essays could be compared to determine if the class has had an effect on the students' impromptu writing.

Having used the approach I've been talking about here in both the teaching of creative writing and composition courses, a few things have become increasingly clear to me. First, the place where students most profoundly face what they see as the mystifying properties of writing is in the activity of revision. Second, the suggestion that it is possible to formulate a group of useful tools that can be used in that context is in itself liberating, in that it both demystifies the process and argues that "learned" mastery is possible. Third, the presentation of the kinds of devices listed above as tools, rather than rules, has strong implications, in that it allows the writer to *use* them rather than be ruled by them. In my experience, as students gain mastery in writing, tools become more and more subjectively defined; in the end, self-sufficiency is reached, and this can be marked by the sense in which the tools students have used have been reformulated and made their own.

Were one to observe a composition class in which the context I have been talking about applied, not much out of the ordinary would be noticed. The teacher would indeed be presenting good writing models, arguing for conformity to basic communal rules, explicating conventions, and—in short—doing the many things that most writing teachers do. Were there differences to be found, they would probably appear most specifically in the course syllabus. There'd be no set number of five-hundred-word themes, no impromptus, no over-prescribed assignments, probably no rhetorical modes approach, and no week-to-week division of work. What might be observed, were the observer to stay long enough, is that from time to time discussion of student work would return to a discussion of intention. This kind of talk would be specific in focus and troublesome and halting in fact. Students would be searching, working to find good reasons for what they had done in very specific situations and working to find ways of doing what they were clear that they wanted to do. During such discussions, I think the class would look at its best the way any practical workshop class would look: the focus would be on materials, on both their pliable and their trenchant properties, and student questions would be, "How can I get this stuff to do what I want it to do?" or "Just what do I want this stuff to do?" What would be good to see is that the questions would be in no way mysterious, though the answers to them might be complex and exploratory as students began to work at the material of their writing. It would be a class without that basic bewilderment present in situations where the materials themselves are experienced as foreign.

Language is not foreign to our students, but too often composition classes seem to be asking students to do something totally new to them. What that might be is hard to figure, but we have all seen it experienced as such early in the semester. What I have tried to do here is to present a way for students to "look into" what they already possess, our language, and in so doing to increase their practical mastery in its use. When things work out, that mastery will be truly *theirs* and not ours; maybe then they'll find what creativity is.

2

Revision:

Another Look

JOE FITSCHEN

Joe Fitschen teaches creative writing and philosophy at Lassen College in Susanville, California. In 1973-74 he received an NEH grant to compare the language models of Wittgenstein and Chomsky, and in 1981 he attended an NEH Summer Seminar on theories of teaching composition.

The etymology of "revision" yields two meanings: seeing anew and putting a new face on things. In the teaching of writing, as well as the practice, it's the second sense that has received the most attention. The piece of writing is regarded as something like a still photograph which needs touching up in the darkroom. Accordingly, we polish, edit, proofread. Sometimes we also find it necessary to reorganize our material, so we cut and paste and add the necessary transitions. Important as these aspects of revision are, those who have focused on writing as process have suggested that revision ought to begin with seeing things in a new way. However, when something is seen from a different perspective, meaning changes, and it seems to me that some of the connections between meaning and the changes one might make in the process of revising are not well understood. As a result, a good deal of what students have been taught about revising, and writing in general, is at least potentially misleading.

We should begin our revising, then, by seeing anew, but the phrase itself contains an informative ambiguity. In one sense, it can be an invitation to see the subject matter in a new way. From this point of view, our model of writing becomes more like a motion picture than a still photograph. We move around the subject, trying new angles and points of view. Usually our coming to regard something in a new light stems from obtaining new information that doesn't fit conveniently into the old scheme. The kinds of changes that this will lead to will vary according to the purpose of the piece, but the writer should at least be in the position of choosing among alternatives. Which details should be included and which left out? Which facts are the most relevant? Which factual claims are the most likely to be accepted as such? Which potential explanation explains the most? Which points are the most informative? Which ideas are the most provocative? To answer questions such as these, whether consciously or intuitively, is to define not only the subject but also the writer's relation to the subject.

The other side of "seeing anew" is an invitation to see the writing itself in a new way. The writer must recognize that language leads a life of its own quite apart from the writer's thoughts or intentions, and so he must find out not only what the writing says but what it implies, what feelings it generates, and what connotations and nuances it contains. The way a particular idea or piece of information is expressed will both limit and provide hints for what else can be said. Clearly, there is no point in polishing and editing until the changes suggested by seeing anew in both senses have been made. The most important point is that such changes are far from being cosmetic. Those that evolve from reconsidering the subject ultimately reflect the writer's values and, along with them, his vision of the world. On the other hand, the changes that come from reviewing the writing should be based on the writer's intentions for the piece of writing. A concern for meaning and esthetic values should control the revision at this level, but neither the writer's intentions nor the words' meaning is always readily identifiable. We can, however, try to come to a clearer understanding of how language works, and this, in turn, should help us make better decisions when we revise. Before expanding on this theme, I would like to set the stage by first examining the role of rules and standards in writing and, second, considering some of the differences between incompetent writers and competent writers (including teachers).

Rules and Standards

Traditionally, spelling, grammar, and punctuation have been regarded as being governed almost completely by prescriptive rules or standards. In spelling, for instance, we have a rule that *i* comes before *e* except after *c*, and then there are a few exceptions like "neighbor" where we appeal to the standard found in the dictionary. In the areas of spelling, grammar, and punctuation, mistakes are usually distinguishable from non-mistakes, and, furthermore, the preponderance of rules and standards that make this possible can themselves be taught. Thus, it's comparatively easy to teach these aspects of writing. Furthermore, such teaching leads to more or less measurable improvement. Matters of organization are not so clearly rule-governed, but one can see in the teaching of the five paragraph theme, an insistence on the topic sentence, and the banishment of the passive voice an attempt to codify organization and structure at different levels. Unlike the case of spelling, however, following such rules does not automatically produce the happiest result, nor have rules been developed for even some of the more common decisions. For instance, when two pieces of information are fairly closely related (and how do we determine *that*?), we may express them as two separate sentences, as a compound sentence, or as a complex sentence. From another point of view, when we encounter a run-on sentence, it might appear as a clear rule violation, but insofar as we cannot tell whether the period or the conjunction has been omitted, it can violate only a rule like: write no run-on sentences. In such matters, to figure out what we should do, we have to consider meaning and esthetics.

At the level of "thought" itself, it might be supposed that there are logical rules; however, the most important group of logical rules for the the writer are the informal fallacies, those concerned with the relevance of evidence—*ad hominum,* begging the question, and appealing to the masses—and those which in one way or another turn on an ambiguity. But these differ from the rules of spelling and punctuation in that they are more concerned with specifying what should not be done than with indicating directly what should be done. And even when no fallacies have been committed and the structure of the argument is valid, a line of thought is frequently flawed by a false premise, and surely the line between the true and the false is not drawn by a rule. We can specify when and why a premise is irrelevant, inadequate, ambiguous, or vague, but a good premise seems to be one which simply does not have these defects. Consequently, many philosophers have traditionally thought of informal logic as being insufficiently rigorous, and when one talked about the "rules of thought," one had in mind formal logic, and, in the last century, symbolic logic. But the application of these rules, which are concerned only with the formal validity of deductive arguments, usually requires translating a passage in ordinary language into a symbolic language amenable to the rules, and there are no rules for accomplishing this. In short, the rules of logic cannot *generate* sound reasoning (or good writing). They function more as warning signs that one's reasoning may be flawed, and what would turn such a flawed argument into a sound one has to be decided on a case-by-case basis.

The point here is that rules of the kind one usually associates with English or logic teachers have an important but still rather peripheral role in writing and revising. They tend to mark the boundary between the permissible and the impermissible but are of little help in distinguishing between the cogent and the tangential, the mundane and the sublime.

The Intuitions of Competent Writers

The result of all this is that revision is frequently necessary even though no rules have been violated, but then it becomes more difficult to specify the grounds for making productive changes. This leads to the difference between competent and incompetent writers. For the most part, competent writers revise intuitively. That is, some aspect of the writing is simply judged to be not quite right, and so alternative versions are tried out until an acceptable one is found. Although the writer usually does not consciously ask specific questions about his writing except in especially sticky situations, the sense of what is going on in intuitive revision can be indicated by questions. Does this idea follow from what has come before? Is this the right (best) word? Has the tone or tense shifted? What about rhythm? In some situations it's difficult even to form questions which might lead to improvement (how might one actually answer the last question?). At the same time, competent writers frequently revise intuitively in those areas where rules are said to govern: spelling, punctuation, and grammar. "Something's not right. There, that's better." To say that a rule governs behavior is not to say that the rule is necessarily appealed to, even unconsciously.

It's not enough to say the difference between the competent writer and the incompetent writer is that the latter lacks this intuitive sensibility in the same measure. Not only do incompetent writers fail to recognize aspects of their writing that need to be changed (this by definition), but often they cannot understand why something needs changing, and therefore they have difficulty making effective changes. It's one thing to point out to a writer that a certain idea lacks any clear connection to the preceding ideas or that the tone or language is inappropriate or that a particular word is misleading or vague; it's another thing for the writer to grasp adequately what this means, let alone generalize from the specific case to similar cases. Yet this must take place before the writing can be improved, and these are aspects of writing which, unlike rules, cannot be directly taught. In short, the thinking which controls the revising process is quite different for the competent writer than it is for the incompetent writer, and yet the teaching of revision is almost necessarily modeled on guesses as to what underlies the activities of the competent writer.

At this point I should admit that my distinction between competent and incompetent writers is quite artificial in that the judgment really has meaning only relative to particular aspects of writing. Some writers who would be judged almost illiterate by the more conventional standards are remarkably direct and concise in their expression and exhibit a strong sense of tone, even though it might operate within a limited range. Other writers who always did well in English classes and even have nice handwriting consistently produce mushy and flat prose. With respect to any particular aspect of writing, then, the competent writer revises, in the traditional sense, with an eye to taking care of the occasional mistake or lapse of judgment or taste, and, on the positive side, looks for ways to improve what is already adequate—better examples, more specific or evocative language, additional ideas. The incompetent writer, however, does not understand how many aspects of language can make a significant difference, or else is unable to make significant judgments about a particular case, which may amount to the same thing.

A Functional Approach

The writing teacher, then, is put in a very difficult position. The intuitions on which the competent writer relies cannot be directly taught, and yet many aspects of revision, one might even say the most important ones, are not covered by the kinds of rules which have traditionally been taught. It may be that truly remedial students have to be given a heavy dose of rules in order that their writing be at least intelligible, but beyond that it seems to me that in order to develop the necessary intuitions what could be called a functional approach works best in the long run.

To understand the functional approach to developing intuition, one might consider one of the differences between intuitions and rules, namely that we can ask for justification or support of an intuition but we need not ask the same of a rule. This is because useful intuitions are connected to an understanding of the functioning of a system, whereas rules are simply followed or applied. That is, if one were asked to justify the use of a rule, all one would have to do is show that it is a bona fide rule that applies to cases of the kind in question. One might be asked to justify the *adoption* of a rule, but this would amount to being asked to justify an *intuition* to the effect that the rule is useful or effective. The point is that such justification of intuitions (insofar as they themselves do not appeal to rules) must consist of reasons why one version functions better than alternative versions. That is, there is a difference between learning the rule that a comma should follow an introductory dependent clause and understanding the difference it makes to a reader when the comma is there as opposed to when it is not—that is to say, understanding its function or role.

The understanding of a system, which allows for justified intuition, is harder to come by than behavior in accordance with a rule, but the flexibility of language and the uniqueness of each piece of writing would seem to demand as much understanding and intuition as possible. In other areas of the efficient industrial culture, design and execution can become separate functions—the carpenter need not understand why he is asked by the architects to do things in certain ways—but such specialization is unlikely, even undesirable, in writing. The adequate understanding of any system includes not only knowledge of the parts and the way they relate to each other, but also knowledge of what will likely happen when some part of the system breaks down. We need to understand both function and malfunction. The way we learn this in writing seems not much different from the way we learn this in other areas. We see, clearly as we can, what happens in particular cases, and as the cases accumulate, we begin to form some tentative generalizations. And we especially note exceptional cases.

The generalizations I have in mind are not the same as rules in that, while they state what is frequently the case with language, they do not prescribe what should be done. For instance, there's a rule that items in a series should be of the same class and also should be similar in form, and there's a generalization that topic sentences, especially at the beginning of paragraphs, help orient the reader and provide coherence among the paragraphs. An exception to the items-in-a-series rule is a violation, but an exception to the topic sentence generalization might be an improved paragraph. The distinction between generalizations and rules is important, I think, not only as a means of resisting unnecessary and undesirable codification with its resultant rigidity, but also because generalizations, properly understood, promote thought, whereas rules do not. Since generalizations, however, do not automatically lead to the best possible text, it is crucial that the writer receive frequent, informed, and specific feedback, not only in terms of conforming to standard English but also in terms of the writing's effect on the reader.

A functional approach, then, sees writing as choosing among alternatives *and* the justification of the chosen alternative. Time was when students were told not to begin a sentence with *and* or *but*. To do so would be to violate an established rule. Unfortunately, the rule did not conform to the practice of competent writers. So students were told they, too, could begin sentences with *and* or *but*. But not every sentence beginning with *and* or *but* works the way competent writers make it work. That is, one cannot split just any compound sentence at the comma without the risk of writing inferior prose. Yet, how would one formulate a rule to govern permissible splitting? One would have to refer to intended meaning, which cannot be rule-governed. One can note, though, that sentences beginning with a conjunction emphasize the conjunction, or that they give more emphasis to what follows the conjunction by virtue of its being connected with what comes before (*and* becomes more like *and not only that . . .*), or they can suggest irony. And no doubt there are other uses for the technique. The point is that one should not use it without some idea of what it might accomplish—that is, without intending it to affect meaning.

One of the consequences of a functional approach as opposed to a rule-following approach is that the former, but not the latter, promotes self-teaching. To understand some of the functions of some of the aspects of language suggests that others can be understood, and the writer can pursue this independently. Again, feedback is necessary, but the writer needs not only the response to his writing, he needs to wonder why his writing elicits (or fails to elicit) particular responses. In one way or another, the answers, even though they are probably not explicitly formulated, will subsequently inform not only the writer's mechanics but also his style or voice, his sense of rationality, and his control of affective responses. On the other hand, it's unlikely that learning rules will lead to the independent development of new rules. The functional approach also explicitly acknowledges the function of a piece of writing as a whole as well as that of the various parts. Indeed, if one does not know what the whole is about, the function of the parts is at best ambiguous.

Put this way, the point seems all too obvious, and yet a good deal of revision, and, one suspects, the teaching of revision, proceeds seemingly oblivious of the writing's reasons for being. This suggests that the priorities for revision should be different from those often taught and especially from those most commonly practiced. The first concern should be with meaning. Does the paper say what one wants to say? And, of course, to answer this question it's necessary that what is said is said clearly. Also, to answer this question the writer needs to be aware not only of what his words actually say but of the more plausible implications of what is being said. Not all connections between sentences or ideas are of the logical type, but writing frequently breaks down because of a faulty connection between what is implicit at one point and what is explicit at another, whether or not the connections are logical in the strict sense. Connotation, the telling detail which suggests others, and even the way rhythm or stress can affect meaning can establish non-logical connections or, on the negative side, lead to something like a contradiction or a non sequitur.

One way the writer can avoid these problems is to claim that he intends nothing beyond the literal meaning of the sentences, but this is to reduce language to its most simple utilitarian level, one that may be aimed at in technical reports or journalism. But even in these cases the way language is used may frustrate the writer's attempt toward neutral objectivity, as can be seen in the revealed, but unconscious, bias of many school newspaper articles.

Meaning and Intention

Considerations such as these lead directly to questions about meaning itself and its relation to what the writer intends. The complexity of these concepts is more than can adequately be discussed here; however, it seems to me that ordinary accounts of meaning are inadequate and frequently misleading, especially for theories of writing.

It's often thought that words acquire meaning by virtue of the things they stand for, whether actual things, according to some theories, or ideas, according to others. From this position it's also easy to see language as a shadow of reality (which is why Swift's philosophers gave it up and carried the real things around on their backs) or as a code designed to convey thoughts. In either case, language is reduced to a medium rather than being acknowledged as a distinct activity which to a large extent generates and structures both reality and thought.

In lieu of a full analysis, a few points about meaning can be suggested. One is the philosopher Wittgenstein's point that the meaning of a word is a function of the use to which it is put. In this regard it's important to realize that use is determined not just by the linguistic context of the word—the sentence, or the piece of writing as a whole—but by the whole relevant human situation. This is more apparent in speech where the speaker and the listener are engaged in other meaning delimiting activities besides talking and listening, but it holds in writing as well. For example, when a product is advertised as being different from its competitors, the consumer is expected to regard that difference as significant in terms of his own needs and desires. That is, in certain contexts we use "different" to mean not only "not the same," but "not the same and therefore better." Similarly, the meaning of "nice" in "It's a nice day" changes somewhat depending on whether it's been nice for weeks or it's the first such day in a month.

Another point is that the meaning of a sentence is a function not just of its components and their relations but other sentences that go along with it, whether or not they are explicitly stated—that is, what one could also be expected to say. This is most easily seen in the logical concept of entailment, but it's not restricted to logical connections. A writer's failure to understand this more extended aspect of meaning is frequently revealed when the writing teacher says, or wants to say, "but . . . but you can't mean that." The sentences hang together if taken literally in their narrowest sense, perhaps, but they manage to do so at the expense of implicitly denying pieces of common knowledge or common sense that provide the background of any piece of writing. This can happen at different levels, but perhaps the most obvious cases are created by those idealists who construct utopian social systems while disregarding even their own experiences as human beings. Another problem, ambiguity, can be analyzed as stemming from the writer's unawareness of differing contexts in which the reader might interpret the text. A writing teacher describes such an experience with the following introductory sentence to a student paper:

Next semester I am transferring to another college because of my experience this semester with a counselor.

Only after reading well into her paper was I completely clear that a Temple counselor had not brutalized K, somehow causing her to change schools. Rather, the counselor had advised her that a degree in biology would be worthless on the job market, and as a result of that advice, K had decided to transfer to Holy Family College where she could get a . . . Bachelor of Science in Nursing . . . *

The writer must always consider what he has to say in the light of what the reader might say and think in the same context. Of course, if the context is established as poetic or expressive, then what one can meaningfully say is different. If no such context is established, however, problems can arise not only with ambiguity, but with contradictions and personifications as well, as in these confusing or imprecise examples from student papers:

*R. Ogle, "Saying What You Mean/Meaning What You Say: Unintended Implications in Basic Writing Papers," (Paper delivered at the Northeast Modern Language Association Annual Meeting, Erie, PA, April, 1983), p. 8.

Since it's a true story it sounds like it really happened.
Society likes smiley people.

A third point is that while what I say (the word's meaning) should conform to what I intend (my meaning) this conformity is not easy to achieve. This is because most intentions are revealed in sentences, and as soon as we have the sentence, questions about the meaning of its words as opposed to "my" meaning can again arise.

To approach this from a different direction, we are frequently tempted to make a rigid distinction between ideas (what we intend to say) and the sentences which express them, perhaps because we think that ideas are mental and private and that the writer's job is to get the sentence to match the idea. This is misleading in that it suggests that ideas lead some kind of independent existence, perhaps something like the architect's drawing as compared to the finished structure. But while we can use the drawing as a standard for judging the structure, drawings and structures exist quite independently of each other, while ideas and sentences do not. To say that one cannot exhibit an idea as one can a drawing because ideas are mental and private is simply to evade the issue, since one cannot exhibit an idea in its purity even to oneself. I might lock up secret drawings that no one else ever sees, but ideas are not like that. To say that a given sentence adequately expresses one's particular idea is to say no more than that one is willing to use the sentence.

Logicians use the terms "proposition" or " statement" to refer to what a sentence says. This allows us to point out that two or more propositions can be expressed by the same sentence (ambiguity) and that two or more sentences can be used to express the same proposition (e.g., active vs. passive voice). It's well to keep these things in mind when revising, of course, but the main point here is that "proposition" is essentially synonymous with "idea," except that propositions are not thought of as essentially private and personal. Insofar as "proposition" can carry the freight of "what is meant, intended, being conveyed" as well as can "idea," it would seem that ideas must, as propositions certainly do, get their life and meaning from the communal enterprise of using language. It's not our direct experience of ideas that gives rise to the concept of ideas (unlike our coming to have a concept of iguanas), but rather our ability to form novel, yet meaningful (capable of being used), sentences.

Speakers can also form sentences that will be considered meaningless by others in their community, though not by themselves. It's important to note that, in such an instance, while it's sometimes appropriate to tell the speaker that he did not say what he thought he said, we cannot tell him that he did not think what he thought he thought. This is because people can't think their thoughts; they can only think. At the same time, if he did not say what he thought, what did he say? And what did he think? Well, we know what he said, what the words were. As to what he thought, we have to assume he *was* saying what he thought, only in some obscure way, unless he was lying, parroting, or simply babbling.

Still, for some reason we expect ideas or thoughts to be more coherent and consistent than language. At least, when we are confronted by a piece of language that does not make sense, we tend to give the speaker or writer the benefit of the doubt. What he *meant* probably makes sense; it's just that the language got in the way. However, with the possible exception of Freudian slips, for the speaker or writer the revised version of his sentences that makes sense to us and the one that does not are in some sense identical if he is willing to use them both in the same context. The difference is that one version works for the audience and the other does not (except in the case of of meaninglessness, where there can be no alternative version).

I once heard a child say to his father upon finally finding his way out of a campground restroom, "I was going the wrong way to the bathroom." A curious turn of phrase, and the more curious it becomes when you try to analyze it. Yet it became clear what the child was saying, that is, what he meant, as I reconstructed the context of his situation. I also thought back to what it's like to be a child. I take it that the child said what he thought. That in the process he violated a number of conventions is another matter. It is just in this kind of linguistic behavior that the distinction between thought and language lies, not in something mental which underlies it. Most of the time we simply speak (or write). Thought is not some essentially separate and hidden process which necessarily precedes speech. Rather, I speak to myself (and I can, of course, say to others what I say to myself) and then accept it or reject it, use it in public or not, regard it as the beginning or the end of a train of thought. If you want to say, "But thought *is* mental," I would agree that this, indeed, is the way we talk about it. That there are thoughts and there are sentences is a lesson in language use, not psychology—in the way language structures our experience, not in the way our minds are organized.

The movement away from ideas as governing language use has led some modern linguists, like Noam Chomsky, to suggest that a good deal of language is governed by a system of rules, perhaps similar to the rule structure underlying computer languages, but this is at best a convenient supposition if one aims to account for all language use. Language is not only behavior, rule-governed or not; it is intentional behavior. And the concept of intentions, like that of ideas, entails their being mental, private, and personal, and they cannot be said to be governed by rules (or not governed by rules either). But to identify an intention we need more than its expression. If someone said he had a particular intention but never behaved (nonlinguistically) as if he had it, we would be justified in doubting him. It is in just this respect that good intentions pave the road to hell. The speaker need not even be insincere. Over the short run he might be simply mistaken, although actual cases of this kind are no doubt rare.

Considerations such as these provide a partial explanation of why students often maintain that their writing says what they wanted it to say even when the instructor claims it does not. The problem is not that the student is failing to match the language to some separate idea, but that (forgive the barbarism) he is "languaging" weirdly. I think students (and others) are doing this often when we might say they are thinking weirdly, too, at least when the problem is not just a matter of logic. On this analysis, then, the writer must not worry so much about what his words mean, in the sense of their corresponding to ideas, but about what they could mean to an audience. The communal aspect of language again. But the familiar requirement that the language should be geared to the audience also needs to be more clearly understood. It tends to suggest that a particular audience is something specific, static, and, with respect to the writing, relatively passive, perhaps like a disease which requires a particular treatment. Or sometimes, perhaps, the audience is thought of as a consumer: he acquires something from the writer, ingests it, and as a result, subsequent changes take place inside him.

There's some point in talking about communication in these ways, but they tend to obscure the similar roles played by the writer and the audience. This is most clearly seen in conversation, where the roles of speaker and audience alternate, and the language is like a ball passed between them. Even thinking of the roles as clearly alternating tends to ignore that what one says in conversation is as much a function of what the other person says and does as it is a function of the "contents" of one's own mind. Conversation is more like tennis, with no clear distinction between offense and defense, than it is like football.

Writing resembles conversation more than is often thought, partly because the good writer tries to second-guess the reader's response, since he cannot actually receive it, especially in persuasive writing. However, except in special cases such as letter writing, the writing audience is a convenient abstraction which can have whatever characteristics the writer chooses, a sort of self-made alter ego for testing ideas. Not only should the writing take place in the figurative presence of an audience, but good writing should also tell the reader how he is expected to respond and adjust to different kinds of writing (kinds being determined in large part by function: to tell a story, to explain, to persuade, etc.). Put another way, the audience referred to in writing texts is not a group of actual readers. Rather it's more like an ideal reader, ideal for the particular piece of writing; and for the writing to accomplish its primary function it must also guide the actual reader toward the state of the ideal reader.

The point here is not to revert to a Platonic world of forms, but rather to stress that the reader must change in certain respects to be able to understand and judge any particular piece of writing. The necessary change can be thought of as a set of expectations. We do not expect puns and symbols in an analytic piece, nor are the facts of the case necessarily the most important part of a description or a reminiscence. When we read poetry we expect sound and rhythm to be more important than in prose. What the particular expectations are is determined by the perceived function of the piece, and a good part of the incompetent writer's difficulty lies in his unfamiliarity with the variety of ways in which language can function.

Again, language can lead a life of its own and say things and perform tasks which no one ever intended. Unfortunately, incompetent writing tends to give us more information about the writer than the writer's subject. The pity is that this "information," much of it damaging, is sometimes false, in that poor writing is not a particularly reliable measure of intelligence, expertise, or effort. Furthermore, seen cumulatively, the actually accomplished tasks in a piece may not be consistent with each other, thereby making unreasonable demands on the reader. For instance, there is a tendency to use personal anecdotes in attempts to persuade. The anecdote can be quite interesting in its own right, but it runs a serious risk of being irrelevant to the argument unless it functions as a clarifying example.

If it's acknowledged that the reader is actively involved not only in deriving meaning from a piece of writing but also in establishing significance and, in some cases, being moved by the piece, then it can be seen that if the writer's intentions are to be realized, more is involved than the transfer of content. When the student insists that he has said what he wanted to say, the teacher might respond that he has managed to say, imply, or evoke, more than he intended, and it is the extra content that leads to contradiction, confusion, or bathos.

Revision for Students

The meaning of one's writing, then, what the language says, should be the writer's first concern in revision. The writer should try to see clearly what his sentences say (or do not say), both explicitly and implicitly. To help the writer do this, teachers and others should carefully explain to the writer just how the words, phrases, sentences, and paragraphs might be construed. It's important that teachers be sensitive to possible meanings and inferences that do not immediately occur to them. Utilizing the reactions of other students is often helpful, but teachers especially should try to represent a wide range of readers, not just themselves. Ultimately, the job is to inculcate certain habits of mind, ones which look for alternatives in both the world and language, and which then make reasoned (or seasoned) judgments among them. In this light, the writing at hand serves primarily as an example rather than as an end in itself.

Once the writer is reasonably clear about the likely meaning of his sentences, he must then decide whether he is willing to lay claim to what is said. It may even happen that the writer decides that what he has said is better than what he intended to say, because not all reasonable meanings of words or implications of assertions are clearly apparent to us as we write. However, even when a sentence, seen in its context, says what one is willing to say, there's still the possibility that it may be misunderstood because we cannot expect all actual readers to be ideal readers. Potential ambiguity is more common than is generally realized. It just so happens that in good prose the context usually pushes us so strongly toward a particular meaning that alternate meanings do not even suggest themselves. Ambiguity is not the only source of misunderstanding, of course. The reader may also draw the wrong inferences, or miss the point of an example or anecdote, or fail to catch the satiric tone. And it would also seem that as we try to increase the amount of meaning in our writing, and also when we move away from familiar territory, the dangers of being misunderstood increase.

To resolve problems of meaning, it's frequently necessary to make changes in vocabulary, spelling, punctuation, grammar, syntax, and even in tone, rhythm, and organization, but the writer should come to understand when such changes significantly affect meaning and when they are more a matter of style. In some cases two words might be sufficiently synonymous so that the meaning does not change regardless of which is used, but in other contexts the choice between the same two words, e.g., "average" and "normal," "writing" and "composing," "football" and "soccer," will affect meaning. Once the writer is satisfied with the meaning of what he has in fact said, then he can further consider such matters as stylistic changes, which may affect the reader's attitudes or feelings, though not the concrete message. Again, this may involve changes in grammar, syntax, vocabulary, and the like, but for quite different reasons from those related to meaning.

A case can be made for saying that any change results in a change of meaning. This is especially true for poets, but here I have in mind the more pedestrian forms of writing where we would acknowledge different ways of saying the *same* thing. The reason for making the distinction between meaning and style is first to show the writer that once he has said *what* he wants to say, the job is not necessarily over; he needs to consider *how* he says it. Second, the writer needs to be warned that as he makes stylistic changes he risks changing the meaning, and, again, this may be advantageous. In short, messing around with the language is one good way of seeing things anew. And finally one can proofread.

To accomplish all of this, I can think of no convenient substitute for actual dialogue between the student and the teacher. This requires a great deal of time, but written comments, assuming they are read, are frequently not understood or are misunderstood because of their condensed form. What *is* frequently understood is that the teacher wants something changed, rather than any deeper comprehension of why. In dialogue, the reasons can be spelled out. The teacher can also suggest many more alternatives, leading the student to come up with some of his own, and then the alternatives can be compared as to the effects they are likely to produce on particular kinds of readers. A nice consequence of this is that if the student understands the differences among alternatives, the teacher is obligated to accept the student's ultimate choice. It may not have been the teacher's choice, but then it isn't his paper either. Also, dialogue means that the student does a good deal of the talking, and this, in effect, is the actual thinking that we can only wish would result from written comments.

Another consequence of dialogue is that the teacher can, and should, try to deal with the student as well as the student's writing. That is, there's a tendency among many students to think it's just their writing that needs to be changed, not themselves. I'm not suggesting here some kind of therapy or self-realization, but rather changes in habits of mind which specifically relate to perception, rationality, sensitivity to language, and esthetic taste. The resultant changes are not the kind that gradually accumulate as the result of much practice. Instead, they appear as quantum leaps typical of new insights and understanding. How one might in practice set the stage for these leaps will vary considerably from student to student and teacher to teacher, but the likelihood of their taking place will increase if teachers keep in mind a broader model of meaning and a corresponding understanding of the multiple roles and functions of language at all levels. As I suggested earlier, the analysis of error or ineffectiveness (malfunction) can tell us much about the nature of language, and writing teachers, more than anyone else, have lots of material to work with. By now we have a great deal of description of these problems; what we need is explanation.

In light of all this it's clear that the process of revising is not at all mechanical. The thought, creativity, and reasoning that went into the first draft must continue all the way through. More importantly, as the revising takes place, it should be accompanied by different mind-sets, and in this regard the distinction, although somewhat artificial, between meaning, style, and mechanics is useful. The relative importance of these elements and the order in which they can most profitably be attacked will vary with the job at hand, although the order in which I have presented them is probably the most usually effective.

In the face of all that I have said so far, it should be remembered how differently people actually go about the task of writing and revising. At one extreme are those who start with free writing and then cut and paste extensively over the course of perhaps a dozen drafts. At the other extreme are those like Bertrand Russell who usually found necessary only a few small changes in his first draft. If we are to come to some better understanding of revising, we cannot generalize from what people actually do when they revise. Rather we must look to the wide variety of *reasons* for making changes which people believe will improve their writing. And even then there will be cases where we have to acknowledge the improvement while admitting that the reason why it works eludes us.

Short of this understanding, we can make use of techniques derived from practice. Such techniques might be quite general, like putting the first draft in a drawer for a week before you revise or reading it to a tape recorder and playing it back; or they may be more detailed like checking all the words over three syllables to see if they can be replaced by shorter words or focusing on general terms with an eye to making them more specific (and a subclass of these techniques may consist of the generally accepted rules). In any case, we must realize that these techniques cannot be expected to apply to all writers or all cases. For this reason we need as many helpful hints about revision, about what can actually make a difference in our writing and why, as we can accumulate.

A final point that I would like to make about revising is a reminder that what we are revising is something that hasn't existed before. That is, I can't pull this sentence out of a drawer to see if the one I've written matches it. Revising is thus not easily differentiated from the creative activity of writing itself.

PART II

The Individual Conference

3

The Individual Conference:

The Psychological Gap

GRACE GANTER

Grace Ganter holds a D. S. W. from Western Reserve, in Cleveland. A professor in the graduate department of the school of Social Administration, she has been at Temple University since 1971. She teaches social and psychological foundations of human behavior to social work students. Her publications include Retrieval from Limbo, *a clinical report of research with emotionally disturbed children and their families, and a social work text,* Human Behavior and the Social Environment, *published by Columbia University Press.*

Different teachers expect students to respond to the learning situation in slightly different ways. These expectations of ours are molded by the particular aspects of behavior to which our attention has been drawn by our own education and experiences. Our explanations of student behavior will differ along with our expectations. We select, out of many possible explanations, those that best explain the teaching-learning situation to us. What we think and feel about the behavior of students, then, is guided both by our expectations and by the explanations we have chosen.

The expectations our students have of us as their teachers follow the same pattern. Their expectations of the ways we will respond to them are also heavily influenced by their previous life experiences as learners. Their previous experiences prepare some students to use our knowledge and competence in their efforts to learn. But some students expect themselves to know what we are prepared to teach them: they experience "not knowing" as a threat to their self-esteem. These students often approach the learning situation with fears of failure. Often, they have not lived their lives in open, supportive environments, and they do not accept the fact that to learn is to have problems and to solve them, to be imperfect and sometimes uncomfortable. At times, we assess them as students whose expectations of themselves are too high. At other times, we view them as defensive about what they do not yet know.

For these students, the individual conference often associated with compostion classes increases feelings of inadequacy. Many of them have encountered people in authority who have accentuated their fears of failure. Frequently, those authority figures did not achieve their positions through knowledge and competence, and they used the power in their positions to make insensitive demands upon young and vulnerable people. Such authorities did not author their own positions, and they could not offer models of maturity with which the students could identify. As actors defined by their positions their transactions with individuals represented a "one-up-one-down" situation. Students whose past experiences have included this kind of encounter may misinterpret our efforts to help them learn in ways we are not always prepared to understand. The individual conference may call up, in these students, images of powerful and dangerous authority figures who somehow control their fates. And we find ourselves asking them to find the words that express their learning needs when the objects of their feelings are these images of us rather than us as we are.

Our efforts to present ourselves to troubled students as sensitive and thoughtful people who respect their right to learn require much more of us than we usually anticipate. Many students are not prepared to take our respect for them on faith; they need time to test the reality of the helping relationship we offer. Testing the reality of this situation makes many demands on both teacher and student, which add to the complications of the individual conference. Since the forms these complications take are perhaps unfamiliar to teachers who have invested most of their time in the classroom situation, let us imagine what might happen with a typical defensive student in conference.

Any student who experiences the individual conference as a confrontation of failure must somehow come to terms with having failed. He or she may see the teacher's judgment as a rejection, not simply of the work at hand, but of him or herself. Having decided to view the teacher as rejecting, the student finds ways of defending against the painful feelings rejection creates. A common defense is self-righteous indignation, which is welcome to the student because it justifies accusation of the teacher as inadequate and punitive. It's as though the thing the teacher has done in confronting the student is the problem. This little bit of defensive magic is based upon the illogic that there was no problem until the teacher pointed it out, and that therefore the teacher has caused it. The feelings evoked by confrontation can make the student quite anxious; the defensive maneuver is an effort to discharge the anxiety by aggressively criticizing the teacher in an effort to make the teacher anxious. If the teacher will take on the anxiety, then the righteous indignation will be justified, and the student need not feel anxious. Unless the teacher can assess the defensive maneuvering, he or she can get hooked into it. It's easy to become somewhat anxious under unfair criticism and to defend in turn by seeing the student as a problem, rather than seeing the student *with* a problem. We frequently do get hooked into this maneuver;

we discuss the "problem students" more often than we discuss students with problems.

If we oblige the student by becoming upset, we tend either to withdraw our energies or to engage in a power struggle which subverts the learning for which the conference was intended. The teacher who withdraws and turns down the student's invitation to engage in an interpersonal power struggle may still have to wait out the student's need to defend in other ways against the threat his or her own inability to write poses. Without a punitive authority to be angry with, the student feels more intensely rejected. Anyone who has experienced feelings of rejection, whether or not they were warranted, can identify the accompanying painful feelings of futility, helplessness, and fear. The student has to try to get into a more active position to feel better. One way is to make a mental reversal: "This teacher doesn't reject me; I reject this teacher."[1] By this means, the student feels more the master of the situation and may now be loath to talk with us at all! We may find ourselves in the position of asking a confused and nonpsychologically-minded person to talk to us about feelings of rejection when we are the object of this rejection. Our chance to increase the student's reality testing is enhanced if we recognize that this rejecting of us creates a new problem for the student. Our own reality is not changed by the student's rejecting us. We have not rejected him or her. The student is dealing in bad faith with that part of himself or herself that is capable of recognizing our reality. We can continue to support the part of the student that is capable of choosing to recognize this. At times, we can help by simply remembering that there is a part of the student that doesn't want to behave this way.

Of course, the above description doesn't represent all individual conferences with students. For purposes of discussion, it compresses and dramatizes more complications than might occur in any one teacher-student encounter. It's intended to illustrate the kinds of responses that can occur when students experience communication with teachers about their learning problems in very personal ways.

It's no news to teachers who deal with students' difficulties in becoming writers that they often experience failure to master principles of written communication in ways that accentuate doubts and uncertainties about themselves. These can often be dealt with only in the individual conference, and sensitivity to the psychological implications of such feelings is critical to the outcome of the one-to-one teaching situation. It may be useful here to discuss further the reasons why students defend themselves against self-knowledge and some of the implications self-observation has for them as they learn to be writers.

Notes on Common Human Defenses

At first glance, a student's defensive behavior might be seen as representing a deeper personality disturbance than an educator should be asked to handle. Some teachers view the first signs of defensive maneuvering as the only behavior of which the student is capable. It's easy to assume that such behavior is so irrelevant to the purpose of the conference as to be unworthy of further attention. But many educators are also students of human behavior. They assume that the individual is valuable, that all individuals have the potential to think well of themselves, to have faith and confidence in themselves, and that they have the right to struggle to maintain and to fulfill their potential. These educators recognize that the student who loses sight of his or her own worth when confronted with the threat of having failed needs help to relocate it, to experience the self as positive and capable of making the choice to grow through learning. Such understanding leads us to respect the need some students have to defend themselves against their erroneous images of teachers; it leads us to maintain our sense of them as valuable individuals with potential for learning despite their defensive maneuvering, and to give them every chance to work their own way out of their trouble.

Students sometimes endow teachers with characteristics they simply do not have. And they proceed to behave toward teachers as if they had these characteristics. We can understand this because most of us have behaved, at one time or another, as if others wanted to devalue us or deprive us of recognition, only to discover, as we came to know them better, that this was not their intention. The discovery includes knowledge that our own uncertainty about ourselves, our suspicion that we might not be very good, or worthy of recognition, was temporarily displaced onto these others. The "as if" assumptions about other people's motives are frequently the result of the desire to avoid painful knowledge about the self.[2]

It's quite true, of course, that people sometimes do deprive us of recognition and that the feelings we experience come from outside ourselves. But whether the problem is inner or outer, we experience fear for ourselves. Abraham Maslow, a psychiatrist who has discussed some of the problems of realizing one's self-potential, observed that,

> ... inner problems and outer problems tend to be deeply similar and to be related to each other. Therefore, we speak simply of fear of knowledge in general, without discriminating too sharply fear-of-the inner from fear-of-the outer .... This kind of fear is defensive, in the sense that it is a protection of our self-esteem, of our love and respect for ourselves. We tend to be afraid of any knowledge that could cause us to despise ourselves or to make us feel inferior, weak, worthless, evil, shameful. We protect ourselves and our ideal image of ourselves by defenses, which are essentially techniques by which we avoid becoming conscious of unpleasant or dangerous truths.[3]

Students who experience the teacher-student relationship as threatening are fearful that they will learn something that will cause them to feel inferior. Although fear of failure is a natural part of life experience, it's an unpleasant part. It can threaten the self-image one wishes to maintain, and protective defenses make it possible to avoid becoming aware of the fear. Many students don't want to know about their fear of failure. It's as though they cannot bear to observe this fear in themselves. Some students have had little opportunity to develop their capacity for self-observation; their life experiences may have discouraged use of this capacity. As educators, we should value our own ability to engage in self-observation and encourage our students to develop it.

In my view, students of writing are especially vulnerable to self-doubts and uncertainties because written communication frequently demands self-expression associated with self-observation. Their vulnerability is associated with this goal of self-observation, so further discussion of the concept may help to clarify the point.

The Capacity for Self-observation

Self-observation requires the ability to distinguish patterns in one's behavior and experience. It "requires the ability to learn to formulate a conception of oneself-as-actor influencing, as well as experiencing, situations of which one is a part . . . "[4] It suggests an awareness of one's own self-boundaries, which define where one's self ends and other selves begin.

In order to see patterns in one's own life experiences, one needs to be free to reflect on them, and to distance oneself from them. To do this well demands that the person be at quite a high level of development, able to abstract certain common behaviors from concretely diverse experiences at the same time, and to generalize from them. Many of our students are more "outer" than "inner" directed, and such introspection is quite difficult for them.

Some students may also be subject to another handicap associated with their experiences with people in authority.

> All self-observation involves some elements of seeing oneself through the eyes of others who have been important in one's life. If these significant others are persons one has admired and liked, then the self-observation develops out of experience that one has felt as positive and supportive. But if [these others are] feared and felt to be unjust . . . the effort becomes more difficult.[5]

Some of our students lack standards by which to look at themselves. They have not been encouraged to find out who they are and what they are like. They have not had enough experience with adults who cared about them, encouraged them to care about themselves, or respected their right to learn from their experiences.

Students who avoid introspection frequently cannot find the words that express their feelings. We notice this in our efforts to communicate with those whose written work does not communicate what they tell us they thought they were communicating. They seem to struggle to find ways of saying something while not saying it. Their ideas are not connected with each other in ways that give us opportunity to help them with self-expression, and they may find it quite difficult to discuss with us what they mean by what they say. It's as though they cannot stand behind their words.

> For a person to be able to "stand behind his words," some attitudes and feelings must gain ascendancy over others. It is the inability to resolve conflicting thoughts or feelings into some unified concept that makes it impossible for some people to speak to the point.[6]

We may notice this in students who find it especially hard to find the words which belong to their feelings about tenderness and anger. They may resist allowing themselves to become aware of tender feelings, because past or current conflicts make tenderness more poignant than they can bear, and the terms in which anger has been experienced and labeled by others in their lives may be too frightening to express.

When we ask students to observe themselves as writers and to take responsibility for what they have communicated, we may be asking some of them to learn to stand behind their words and resolve conflicting thoughts and feelings. We need to learn to recognize how difficult this can be for those whose life experiences have encouraged them to defend against such behaviors. From the students' point of view, we may be asking them to perceive their lack of self, their inability to separate their observations of themselves from the ways they have been perceived by others. They may experience our concern to help them integrate their thoughts and feelings as an assault on self-esteem. If, then, they do not see their self-expression as worthwhile, they may not see themselves as worthwhile. In this instance, they may be afraid of the knowledge we have to offer because it causes them to feel weak or inferior, and they may protect themselves from these painful feelings.

Teachers who invest their energies in efforts to free up students to use their creative abilities will also recognize that students may defend against knowledge of their creativity. These are students whose ability for self-observation is not at issue: their fear of self-knowledge has other meanings.

The Danger of Creativity

Teachers of writing learn a good deal about the cost to the person of accepting the ability to create something new. Recognizing one's own creativity may bring with it another kind of danger which increases feelings of vulnerability. Accepting one's difference may amount to exposing oneself to criticism. While negative criticism may not come from one's English teachers, it may come from others who enforce normative behaviors through socialization into a society which does not allow much space for free movement of the unusual. Those who deviate from behaviors that are traditionally expected also suffer from feelings of self-doubt and uncertainty. In this sense, people may defend against their human potential, their inner drive toward actualization of the self. According to Maslow, "Everyone of our . . . creators . . . has testified to the element of courage that is needed in a lonely moment of creation, affirming something new (contradictory to the old). This is a kind of daring, a going out in front all alone, a defiance, a challenge."[7]

Most people are not encouraged to realize their human potential. To dare to create something new which differs from what is routinely expected is difficult for a number of reasons. These include social pressures toward conformity to what the majority of people important to the person think, say, and do about what they value in human behavior. It can be quite threatening to perceive things differently from the way others perceive them.

> People like other people to see things in the same way they see them, and tend to aspire to acceptance in groups that will fit the particular mixture of pleasure and pain to which they have become accustomed. To hold an opinion, then, which is different from the opinions of most others is to be alone with one's opinion.[8]

As we ask our students to take on new knowledge of the world, we are asking them to change some of the ways in which they have become accustomed to viewing human behavior, including their own. Taking on new knowledge implies taking in new ways of evaluating one's self. We may encourage students with stereotyped self-images to express some things which they have viewed as "wrong." The knowledge that we teach them to value may run counter to that which is valued by significant others in their lives. If students take on new knowledge, they will need to affirm something new which is contradictory to old beliefs and values still held by people with whom they want to continue to share their lives.

To become persons of their own, then, students have many choices to make which can critically influence their existence. The process of learning concerned with differentiating one's self from others may involve risk which is experienced as vulnerability. The developing self is vulnerable to change in the feelings associated with self-image. Perhaps we should see our students as risk-takers and accept that some of them may find their creative urges to be dangerous. They may not wish to observe themselves as creators in the face of pressures to conform to others' norms. The extent to which they are open to knowledge of their creative potential may well depend on our efforts to explain the nature of choice, of psychological freedom, and of the individual as a chooser.

Summary

The one-to-one teaching situation requires that teachers confront and respond to the psychological implications of students' behavior. Those aspects of behavior to which teachers choose to respond will depend on how they perceive themselves and their students. What teachers view as important to observe in students' behavior is informed by those aspects of behavior to which their attention has been drawn. Frequently, there is a gap between the knowledge teachers have of their subject matter and their knowledge of the psychological significance of a student's behavior. An effort has been made to draw attention to a few critical psychological factors which influence the outcome of the individual conference.

The one-to-one teaching situation is a human encounter. Within it students may experience their failure to meet the teacher's expectations as serious failures in themselves. They may defend against painful feelings associated with this sense of failure in a variety of ways. Their expectations of how teachers will respond to them are heavily influenced by their previous life experiences as learners. Some of them have encountered people in authority positions whose responses to them have exploited their fears of failure. Students need time to test out our willingness to help them learn in ways that differ from their past experience. As they test the reality of the helping relationship we offer, they may continue to endow us with the characteristics of those from whom they have experienced negative responses. Their defensive maneuvering in the face of our efforts to help them is self-defeating for them. But we can easily get hooked into their defensiveness and see them as problems to us rather than as students who have problems.

It's important to remain open to the emotional experiences which students have as they learn, to recognize that all students have potential to think well of themselves, as well as the right to struggle to fulfill their potential. This requires respect for the dignity of the individual student, understanding of the difficulties students may have in realizing their capacities for self-observation, and the acceptance of common human defenses that students may need to use as they work their way through their learning difficulties.

The self-observing capacities of students may not be well-developed, or students may perceive dangers in self-observation related to their fear of knowledge of themselves. Students of writing may be particularly vulnerable to self-doubts, for written communication requires self-expression associated with the capacity for self-observation. Students who avoid introspection often have difficulty making connections between their thoughts and their feelings. Past or present life conflicts may make it especially difficult for them to find the words that belong to feelings of tenderness and anger, against which they may need to protect themselves. Teachers can appreciate the plight of the student who cannot or will not engage in self-observation by keeping in mind their own difficulties in gaining and expressing knowledge about themselves.

Students may also defend against knowledge of their creativity. Teachers of writing learn to recognize that a person's creativity can increase feelings of vulnerability because of social pressures to conform to traditional ways of thinking. Successful efforts to enable students to use their creative potential depend upon our ability to accept those parts of the students that struggle against such social pressures.

Notes

[1] Grace Ganter, Margaret Yeakel, and Norman Polansky, *Retrieval from Limbo* (New York: Child Welfare League of America, Inc., 1971).

[2] Grace Ganter and Margaret Yeakel, *Human Behavior and the Social Environment* (New York: Columbia University Press, 1980), p. 83.

[3] Abraham Maslow, *Toward a Psychology of Being*, 2nd ed. (New York: Van Nostrand Reinhold, 1968), p. 60.

[4] Ganter, Yeakel, and Polansky, *Retrieval*, p. 26.

[5] Ganter, Yeakel, and Polansky, *Retrieval*, p. 65.

[6] Ganter, Yeakel, and Polansky, *Retrieval*, p. 24.

[7] Maslow, *Psychology of Being*, p. 61.

[8] Ganter and Yeakel, *Human Behavior*, p. 66.

4

Some Psychological Implications of Student-Teacher Conferences

LINDA HILLMAN

Linda Hillman is a clinical psychologist at the Bronx Psychiatric Center, where she is on the faculty of the Psychology Department, and is Clinical Instructor at the Albert Einstein College of Medicine. She is also in private practice in New York City. She holds a Ph.D. in clinical psychology from the City Univeristy of New York. Her work involves teaching and supervising trainees in psychology and psychiatry, often in one-to-one settings.

Many of us have experienced both the joy of conducting individual writing conferences which are rich with learning and the frustration of conducting those conferences which are unproductive. While there's no one reason for the success or failure of these conferences, I would like to address a topic which may account for some of the obstacles and frustrations which arise in conducting them. The student's capacity to learn and be helped, including his capacity to accept and use criticism, depends upon certain aspects of his psychological development. In particular, it depends upon the development of his sense of self. For this reason I would like to begin with the topic of narcissism and work toward a discussion of the individual conferences themselves.

The subject of narcissism has been popular of late in mass media, in books by social historians, such as Christopher Lasch's *Culture of Narcissism*, and in the field of psychoanalysis, where a whole new psychology of the self has created great controversy. I will briefly describe some of these recent contributions to the understanding of narcissism.

It's commonly assumed that to accuse someone of being narcissistic is to accuse him of having too much self-love or of being full of himself. While grandiosity is often apparent in a narcissist, it is feelings of worthlessness and emptiness which truly characterize pathological narcissism.

While the narcissist is characteristically self-absorbed, his self-esteem may fluctuate greatly depending on how much admiration he is getting and from whom. Some people in the narcissist's world are idealized and envied while others are deprecated and used. Only those who are envied are seen as having anything worthwhile to give. When these idealized people are inevitably found to be fallible, the idealization dissipates and these same people are seen as contemptible.

How does this happen? According to one theorist, H. Kohut, two parallel developments in infancy are necessary for the realization of healthy self-esteem: the narcissistic self and the idealized parent image.[1] For the development of the narcissistic self, the newborn infant has to feel as if he or she were the center of the world. The mother is not seen as having a separate existence. Therefore, the infant's omnipotence is responsible for all its needs being met. This feeling of self-perfection is the source of the toddler's grandiosity and exhibitionism. In plain language, "Look at me. I can do anything." This grandiosity and exhibitionism is appropriate to the child's stage of life. It only becomes pathological if the nurturing environment cuts it off prematurely or prevents its gradual diminution.

A parallel process to the one just described goes on *vis-à-vis* the idealization of the mothering figure (i.e. the idealized parent image). The mother is seen as omnipotent and able to satisfy all needs. Again, inevitable frustrations in the form of needs not met lead to the gradual diminution of the idealized parental image. An assault on this process may take the form of the parent's being unable to tolerate the child's idealization or being unable to give it up at the appropriate time. Any of these may lead to pathological developments for the child, including a constant longing for an idealized mother.

For our purposes we are concerned only with the first process described, the development of the narcissistic self. Any disruptions in this self lead to feelings of shame. Early traumatic onslaughts of self-esteem lead to the repression of grandiose fantasies before they can be healthily tested and integrated into the ego. One is left with feelings of inadequacy and shame while at the same time secretly harboring grandiose fantasies. For example, a person may do little to promote his career because he expects that the rest of the world ought to know how good he is. Or someone might not work at revising his writing because he harbors the secret, or the not quite conscious belief that his first draft ought to be perfect.

What is particularly important about this way of viewing narcissism is that it separates the development of one's feelings about oneself from the development of relationships with others. Narcissism has its own developmental cycle and healthy narcissism is a prerequisite for a good life. Narcissism in and of itself no longer has purely negative connotations. Someone who is pathologically narcissistic has had a disruption in the course of his or her phase of appropriate grandiosity and idealization. For example, when the infant needed to experience its perfection and omnipotence, the mother might have become overly anxious and acted in a protective manner, perhaps even controlling the infant's movements. Or perhaps the child was abruptly forced, rather than gradually allowed, to experience failure or disappointment. It's important to note that the problem is in the fit between the infant's development and the nurturing environment.

Implications for Teaching

Typically clinicians find that few patients have pure narcissistic character disorders. Rather, many ordinary neurotics have pockets of unresolved narcissistic issues. While teaching at the City University of New York, I met a great many students who suffered severe self-esteem problems. Clearly, the lives of many of these inner-city students were greatly affected by societal traumas which were filtered through family life. School had often become another failure experience where, at best, they had experienced much criticism and little constructive help, and, at worst, had been benignly neglected and pushed through the system. They wind up in college without any of the years of background work necessary to handle even introductory course work. Writing, one of the modes of communication most valued by this culture and certainly one on which achievement and advancement is largely dependent, is among these missing skills. They don't know how to do it and no one has ever helped them learn.

However, it's the rare student who will walk into your office and say, "I don't know how to do it. Please help me learn." In students with the kind of low self-esteem I have been describing, you will see only the defense. That is, you may be verbally attacked for your "so-called wish to help." The vindictive aggression of the narcissist stems from deep feelings of self-hate which are externalized. Or perhaps you will feel ignored, made to feel you don't exist or haven't in any way touched the person to whom you are speaking. The denial of your importance prevents the narcissistic person from being hurt by you.

The true narcissist's distance and disregard can evoke hostile and punitive feelings in the professor, including the wish to humiliate. The narcissist actually elicits just the response he or she most dreads. It's important for the teacher to refrain from retaliation against the student while not allowing himself to be used or manipulated. In order to maintain an empathic stance at such a time, it may be helpful to remember that underneath the student's infuriating behavior is profound vulnerability. Another way of maintaining empathy is to remember a narcissistic blow that you have experienced, a promotion not granted, a paper rejected for publication.

While not specifically writing on the topic of narcissism, D. W. Winnicott describes how the early nurturing environment of the infant and young child can foster or inhibit cognitive development, especially the capacity to learn.[2] According to Winnicott, the capacity to be helped involves an ability to trust. When you are deeply wounded at an age when you did not have the internal resources you have as an adult, you close off the world prematurely while internally remaining more vulnerable. All your energy then goes into protecting yourself from the repetition of such an experience. Despite a teacher's good intentions, such a person may either take in nothing or everything, but remain seemingly untouched by anything.

In order to learn, writes Winnicott, one must be able to take in. However, a state of readiness or emptiness is a prerequisite for taking in. If a child's feelings have been met with no response from a parent, the child is left hanging, the feeling is repressed, and an unpleasant state of emptiness remains. Learning becomes unpleasurable, even feared, since it too is associated with a state of emptiness. To protect himself, such a person creates a state of controlled emptiness, perhaps not taking in, not eating, not learning, or by greedily and indiscriminately filling up in a way that doesn't allow anything to be internalized. While Winnicott is describing severe disturbances, similar issues may be stirred up in all of us without such extreme consequences.

These psychological correlates of learning may have specific behavioral manifestations when the teacher sits down to meet with the student in the individual conference.

The Individual Meeting

What makes the individual meeting different from one in the classroom? In the classroom many students are competing for the instructor's attention. Resources are felt to be scarce and competitors plentiful. In the individual meeting the student has the instructor all to himself. This allows a greater sense of hope that the student's needs may be met.

While there's potential for better student-teacher interaction in individual meetings, there are also potential pitfalls. A teacher's primary task is to teach writing, and this task will be central in the individual meeting. Thus, instead of sitting face-to-face, the teacher and student will be sitting side by side, presumably with a manuscript in front of them. In any interaction (one-to-one or group) there are usually multiple hidden agendas for the participants, whether it's for one to show the other up, for one to seduce the other, or for one to be fed (metaphorically) by the other.[3] In a work situation, one ignores or subordinates these other agendas to the primary work task. The pitfalls for conferences have to do with some of these hidden agendas, which we will now consider, along with ways of managing them.

We live in a culture that highly values independence. "Dependency" has negative connotations. While it's clearly difficult to deal with the passive dependent student, it's also quite difficult to handle the "pseudo-independent" student or the one whose defenses against dependency make him wall himself off from learning. Students who can't allow themselves to learn or to be dependent in the ways that students realistically need to be will react with a wide variety of defensive styles. There's the student who's so frightened of being in the dependent position that he cannot allow himself to attend the individual meeting. This is one of the hardest resistances to overcome. Sometimes if the teacher is able to remain available and encouraging, the student may begin to attend meetings over time. What is most important is that the teacher arrange to have some alternate way to use the time in case the student doesn't show up. This will cut down on the teacher's resentment, and he or she is then less likely to withdraw or be unwittingly vengeful toward the student. The teacher's being consistently available may be just what is needed to help the student connect. On the other hand, the teacher needs to know when to let go of the grandiose wish to motivate every student and to put his or her energy where it will do the most good. If a student doesn't attend classes and meetings over a long period of time, it may be helpful to discuss with the student plans other than continuing in the class.

Among students who do attend the individual meetings, some may argue with the teacher and deny errors, saying they have written just what they intended to write and that the teacher is being too fussy or picking on them. This is another manifestation of narcissism. Anything the student does is right simply because he does it, despite the actual impact his work has on others. Here again, the student who is quite insecure and worried about others' evaluation will deny that this matters to him and revert to an earlier, egocentric mode of functioning. In this situation, the student might induce the teacher to argue with him, but this isn't likely to lead to any positive outcome. If the teacher can validate the student's expression even in its raw form, he may then be able to help the student channel his meaning or "sense of what he wants to say" into more appropriate forms.

If the primary task of the individual meeting is to teach writing, how should the teacher handle the student's attempt to divert him? Often students try to change the student-teacher relationship into a friendship. While this may be gratifying to one or both, it may interfere with the work, as when the student feels betrayed by negative feedback or the teacher reluctant to offer it or feels guilty after doing so. While some people are more comfortable with flexibility in their teacher role than others, the critical factor is whether the teacher is able to put the goals of teaching first.

The intimacy of the one-to-one relationship is what makes it more likely for the student to trust the teacher. However, if the teacher is warm and supportive, the student might want her to be more of a therapist or confidante than a teacher. The student who pours out his innermost problems may be doing so for many reasons. He may want sympathy or special treatment, or to avoid working; or he may simply want help and have no one else to turn to at that moment. For students with self-esteem problems, a certain amount of empathetic listening may be helpful. However, it's important for the teacher to keep the primary task of teaching writing in mind. At a certain point, a referral for outside help may be indicated. This becomes especially important if advice and reassurance do not seem to help or seem never to be enough, and the student is inconsolable and unable to move back to the task of writing after an appropriate period. Although the teacher might feel guilty about cutting off the student's talking about personal problems, it's ultimately better to channel that discussion in a more appropriate direction (counselling or therapy). It also benefits the teacher-student relationship, for the teacher will feel less resentment about the student's demands.

For those students with the kinds of self-esteem problems described earlier, there are several things a teacher can do to alleviate difficulties. The first is to communicate an understanding of how difficult writing might be for them, how it's unlikely that anyone has really helped them with this in the past, how they feel like failures, and how hard it is to keep on trying. The words chosen must feel comfortable to the particular teacher. Some empathic communcation, if it's genuine, is likely to be very helpful.

Secondly, I would begin by pointing out the positive aspect of the student's work, which all too often can be taken for granted. It would be especially helpful to address areas of improvement. This will help temper the impact of the criticism.

The image described earlier of the teacher and student sitting side by side looking at the work is used to highlight two points. One is the sense that the work, not the person, is being criticized. Any way that this can be communicated is likely to benefit the student. Secondly, it may foster a sense of collaboration. That is, the two of you are working together to improve the student's skills. You are not there to judge or punish the student for failures. If the student must pass a university test, you may be able to use that as your mutual goal.

Finally, it's important to know that what you say may not be what is heard. For students with low self-esteem, your tone or the associations triggered by your words may be given more weight than the content of your communication. I would ask the student at the end of the conference to summarize what was discussed. Listen carefully for the distortions which are bound to be there and try to correct them.

The Teacher's Dilemma

The way in which a university system affects a professor may influence the way the professor deals with the student in the one-to-one meeting. For example, at one large public urban university I know of, a program was initiated to train professors to teach remedial writing. Because of low enrollment in some liberal arts courses and the great need for remedial writing teachers, professors in areas of low course enrollment were asked to teach it. The faculty resented the imposed reapportionment of their time both because of the way it was done and for deeper reasons. After devoting years of work to their areas of specialization, they had to give these up. In addition, they felt that the values and academic standards with which they had been raised had been greatly eroded. Furthermore, they were being asked to teach just those students whom they blamed for this erosion. It would be surprising if there were not some conscious and unconscious resentment towards this project even in the most willing participants, and while these feelings are understandable, they must be addressed if such a project is not to be undermined.

It would also be reasonable to expect this resentment to surface in meetings with students. While no professor would be purposefully sadistic with students, it might be easier and safer to express resentment towards them than towards the university administration. These feelings might take the form of "Why are these students here anyway when they can't manage the work?" Such thoughts might lead to further unwitting humiliation of an already deeply humiliated student.

Looking for someone to blame in this situation is useless. The problems are too complex. But expecting teachers to solve all these problems is another trap. Unrealistic expectations of what can be done to make up for years of improper training and lack of practice can lead to great disappointment. Some students will benefit in large ways, some in small ways, and some not at all from a writing program. To expect otherwise will lead to further frustration and resentment.[4]

Notes

[1] H. Kohut, "Forms and Transformations of Narcissism," *Journal of the American Psychoanalytic Association,* 14 (1966), 243-272.

[2] D. W. Winnicott, "Fear of Breakdown," *International Review of Psychoanalysis,* 1 (1974), 103.

[3] W. R. Bion, *Experience in Groups* (New York: Ballantine Books, 1961).

[4] I would like to thank Kenneth Eisold for his help in formulating some of the ideas in this paper.

5

Student Worlds in Student Conferences

STEPHEN ZELNICK

Stephen Zelnick is an Associate Professor of English at Temple University and has served as Director of College Composition for the past four years. He has attended the Pennsylvania Writing Project's Summer Institute and the Writing Program Administration's Summer Seminars and has published recently on writing program administration in Teaching Writing *and* WPA Journal. *He has also published essays on Defoe, Conrad, Melville, and Fitzgerald and is currently revising an essay on Trollope. He also served as National Coordinator of the Marxist Literary Group and edited the newsletter* Mediations.

Looking out my office window ten stories up, I see Philadelphia as it appears to few others. To my right I see my city's version of Dickens' Coketown, more than a century into its dismal life. From up here, however, the bulky warehouses and dead factories have a kind of grandeur. The caved-in railway sheds are etched over by streaks of electrical lines that play against the narrow-winding streets, where I know hardly anybody lives. Here and there, a square of houses is mostly gone; the lone shell of a single house reminds me that Coketown is dead.

If I turn the chair at my desk one-third of a circle to my right, I look out on a scene that seems made for a poster promoting the city. There is the Delaware River moving far down and away, and two grand suspension bridges down river, the nearer one an expressionist's deep blue. In the foreground is the splendid golden dome of a Ukrainian Cathedral. Over the river is the sad, workaday world of Camden, New Jersey; and looking far downriver on a clear day, I can catch a glimpse of the first promise of the Atlantic.

Directly behind me is the city skyline, but at an unusual, unofficial aspect. At this height and distance, center city is humbled and flattened by the long vistas against which it appears. Those massive office towers, which I sometimes imagine are buzzing and crackling with more electric energies than my poor ivory tower, look squat and dull. Looking there, one names

47

the familiar buildings, but one does not dream of anything.

Over my left shoulder, there is University City (the University of Pennsylvania), and then miles and miles of close-packed residential neighborhoods. Though I know at the end, where the deepest horizon is, are the airport and then the highways down to Washington, from where I see it, the residential prairie seems to go on forever. Beyond the great railroad terminal building and the post office, oversized Greco-Roman temples dedicated to democratic gods, are the vast lands of the working people that go on and on.

Students come to my office to talk about comma splices. They come to have "conferences." I keep the blinds between my double-glazed windows pulled up. These student conferences that have become an essential feature of composition courses are really unusual events. There are no other courses I know about in the university where a professor and a student are locked up, even for a short time, in a room together. Often, too, the terms of this confabulation are not clearly specified, and neither the teacher nor student has a very exact idea of what will happen. Although it's a fairly safe bet that the conference is more tense for the student than the instructor, there is anxiety on both sides.

The student, after all, is in a position of being judged, no matter how homey the office or how dressed-down the professor. The whole purpose of the conference is easily perceived by the student to be a review of the errors in the student's last essay. In addition, the conference occurs in the teacher's territory, where mysteries abound—the official desk and telephone, the long array of book spines, perhaps (as in my case) the secretary (with a friendly/ terrifying "May I help you?") guarding my heavy door. It's the rare student who is not immediately impressed with a sharp sense of juvenility in the face of these signs of power. The loping motions of the younger students are hemmed in within our tight offices; their jeans (even if we are wearing jeans) are out of place; and the backpack is awkward in the world of file cabinets. Students fumble in the depths of whatever serves them as briefcase to find the paper you want to go over, another something to write on, and something to write with, and then where to lean, and how to look, and so on.

I may be revealing a tendency to listen to the grass growing here, but I am always acutely aware of the unease of my students when they come through my door. I am also aware that each one of these conference encounters is full of risks for me. More so than the classes I teach, where the task of bringing order to the immediate experience of twenty-five or so students protects all of us from the strange hidden corners of our personalities, conferences are likely to force some moment of vivid personal exchange. In front of a class, we can perform a public self, but in the close quarters of a student conference, we are pressured to adopt a mask closer to ourselves.

The task is made no less difficult because the teacher is inevitably in the position of explaining why this paper is not an "A." To be sure, we all have a rational grasp of the need for this moment. After all, these students are developing writers, and it is one's task to show and explain the shortcomings in a student's work in order to recommend remedies. This is what the situation demands from us; it is even, supposedly, what the student wants from us. Yet, in obvious human terms, this is unpleasant. Our students give us gifts to admire, and we always say, "This isn't what I wanted." (How often do they remark, "I hope this is what you wanted!")

Other and stranger channels open in our conferences. I don't know whether most students have any other occasions where they meet one-to-one with an adult professional. And there is so much advice and reassurance they want and need from the adult world that they may wish to enter. One gets signals of this all through conference time. Our freshmen want to know whether they are working as hard as college students ought to be, whether they should feel enthusiastic about their work, how they will know whether what they're studying is right for them, whether you're attracted to them (in every conceivable way), and, of course, the mysteries of your life—are you happy being a teacher, do you write books, are you married, do you have children, what do you believe about this and that, are you satisfied with your life? I am afraid that whether we wish it or not, we become role models for our students.

And, finally, there is the romantic/sexual vibration. If it is in any way possible, conferences set going a buzz and flutter of fantasies. Young students, especially, are notorious for their fantasies and unguarded expressions. There is a sweetness and liberality in young people that is terribly attractive, and very easily misinterpreted by adults. Teachers, too, tend to be an odd sort of adult—nurturing people who respond far more readily than most to emotional promptings. The situation is often overripe. For the students, we may become the adults who can teach them many things; for us, they are the youthful drift that is sometimes difficult for us to find in our measured lives. Perhaps that is why those who have written about student conferences have worked so very hard to make these meetings merely technical and mechanical; they have even provided us the clean and clinical term, "conferencing"!

"Conferencing" is an invention of the Writing as Process movement that has had a dramatic and, generally, salutary effect on writing instruction in the last decade. Very briefly—since most of us have learned to march comfortably beneath this banner—writing as process (and not product) asks writing instructors to regard writing as having three stages: prewriting, writing, and rewriting. The least interesting, in this view, is the actual first-draft writing; instead, teachers are asked to accustom their students to think of writing as a process that requires discovery and invention in the formative stage and energetic revision, recasting, and redrafting at a critical later stage when everything that has gone before is tested for public presentation. As the process approach has caught hold, an entirely different pedagogy has emerged in which student conferences have taken on a special significance.

At its very best the student conference is conceived of as an opportunity for the student to gain a necessary perspective for revision. Here is the chance for the developing writer to find a helpful pre-audience while still in the process of bringing the essay out of its private and/or miscast and/or inchoate state into public effectiveness. The very fact of there being this pre-audience available would help the writer view a draft from the perspective of this knowledgeable other. Reading the draft aloud, or listening while the instructor read and puzzled through the essay, or even just observing the reactions of a silent reader would help the writer realize the special problems of effective communication. (See, for instance, Fitschen's paper in this volume.)

Of course, the more obvious and most valuable intervention would be the remarks the instructor could make and the specific advice and exercises the instructor could offer the student on the road to the next revision. The instructor, at best, would have the experience, wisdom, and tact of a Donald Murray[1] so that, while this intervention offers guidance and advice, the student is still left with the critical rewriting decisions. The instructor is not to rewrite the essay but is to guide the student carefully towards a sharp awareness of purpose and audience and to share with the student some of the techniques to enhance communication.

Conceived this way, student conferences were provided a powerfully sensible place in composition pedagogy. But something awful happened in bringing this dainty dish to the table. In the hands of Donald Murray, who would expect anything but happy results from student conferences? Unfortunately, very few of our composition teachers are both practiced writers and experienced teachers—very many are neither one nor the other. Moreover, very few of us (do any of us, these days?) teach in schools like those Murray worked in, where composition classes are limited to a dozen students and, even more telling, to those who arrive in our classes with the high motivation that would allow this classic conception of conferences to work very well. While student conferences have become an essential requirement in the format of most composition programs I know of (indeed, have replaced the classroom as center-stage in many), my observation is that they are going on badly.

First, there are larger numbers of less well-prepared students enrolled in our classes, and classes are often taught by adjunct staff. Moreover, if that were not more than enough already, the status of revision has never been made precisely clear and becomes less so as soon as we leave the intelligent pages of the Donald Murrays. My guess is that for more than three-quarters of the writing teachers at college level, rewriting continues to mean correcting surface errors to improve the grade a student has received, without really recasting the essay. Student essays, thus, will remain first drafts and never be much more than that. The mechanization of the conception of revision follows reasonably from the conditions in which composition is taught.

One reasonable, yet damaging, response has been to make a virtue of these necessities by adopting an assembly-line attitude. The Mel Brooks psychiatrist, Dr. Akiva ben Hollywood, claimed to have treated the entire Israeli army in a single afternoon: he said to each of them, "Hello, how are you? Good-bye, and good luck." There are compositionists who claim a similar efficiency. Roger Garrison advocated spot interventions, which is perhaps a good idea in its limited way, especially at the high school level where it was intended.[2] But by calling this a conference method, Garrison has made it easy for others to supplant the true conference with these rapid encounters. Students write, and bring their writing in the midst of their work to the instructor for instant correction. This approach has all the advantages of instantaneousness—and also all the disadvantages. This emphasis on efficiency has led to the desire to streamline and mechanize what is a somewhat confusing and risky, but significantly personal experience.

This tendency can be seen very clearly in Rosemarie Arbur's influential essay, "The Student-Teacher Conference."[3] Arbur asks us to take a lesson from an interview form used by social case workers. She believes this would be useful since too often our "conferences are undifferentiated, played-by-ear experiences . . . . " Social workers, we are assured, have a firmer grasp of these conference occasions "because the problems they seek to alleviate . . . are usually of far greater human importance than an F on a paper or a D on an exam . . . . " If "we English teachers" would adopt this format, we could "achieve more consistently and effectively the pedagogical purposes that are our special business" (p. 338). The format is a nice bit of people management, the smooth movement of a troublesome client in and out. And it is also neatly task-oriented, so there are no shocks or surprises. Arbur identifies seven stages of the interview: "engagement, problem exploration, problem identification, agreement to work on the problem together, task assignment, solution, and termination" (p. 338). The great gain here is that things go smoothly. Fears and tensions are allayed by calming phrases; a precise focus fixes the specific problem; its precise solution is embodied in specific exercises for the student to do; there are contractual moments throughout; and the student is sent forth to have a nice day.

Arbur's essay is far from worthless, and I have used it for years in training sessions with new instructors to help them develop an awareness of format in their conferences; but borrowing a frame that may work for some social workers has only limited applicability to education. Arbur does remind us that student conferences ought to be purposeful and should provide both student and instructor with a distinct sense of accomplishment and a clear idea of the next step. Who would argue with this in principle? Yet, I am increasingly uncomfortable with these sensible suggestions.

My unease is not only with the professional people-management style of "engagement" and "termination"; I resist also the emphasis on mechanical tasks. I find that this approach identifies the intervention too narrowly and leaves no room for the powerful personal dynamic of the student-teacher relationship, which is itself formed by powerful societal forces. Arbur's essay tells me, in its quite unassuming and sensible way, that the student's writing problems are to be found in some local events in the essay. These local events—let's assume they are such things as problems in sentence continuity, or vague and imprecise verbs, or under-developed paragraphs—are to become the objects of concern in the conference. The teacher identifies the problem, tests the student's recognition of the error, indicates appropriate corrections, tests the student's understanding of these remedies, and assigns further exercises to permit the student further opportunities to recognize and repair the error (and perhaps the student is urged to correct the error-laden essay for a higher grade). What could be more sensible and more likely to produce a keen sense of accomplishment for both participants; and what an efficient use of twenty minutes it is; and how could we better avoid the pathetic dead-stop of the professor lecturing the single head-bowed student on the vague need to write better! Yet, I find I do not run conferences that resemble Arbur's social worker's interview. The source of my students' writing problems is not to be found in local events within the 8½ x 11 boundaries of their essays. Something else is going wrong for them when they write, and the local events are the traces of those larger problems. Conferences, I find, are the only place to explore these deeper issues.

A third, more promising approach to student conferences, an essay I highly recommend, is Thomas A. Carnicelli's "The Writing Conference: A One-to-One Conversation."[4] Carnicelli has investigated the transcripts of taped conferences and has evaluated the recorded conversation in light of the piece of writing being discussed and the possibilities for revision. Carnicelli's regard is intensive, involving a deep analysis of a few typical conferences, rather than a broad study of many. Although, like Arbur, Carnicelli is interested in the mechanics of the interview, he is much more concerned with the roles both participants tend to assume and how these roles frustrate instruction and revision. In the sample conference Carnicelli analyzes in greatest depth, we observe the instructor making the very bad (and very familiar) choice of assuming to know more about what the student-writer wants to say than the writer does. Intervention here becomes a hideous type of intrusion, where we as teachers feel we must be superior in understanding experiences and feelings even though they are not ours. With leading remarks like "don't you really want to say," or "isn't this more important," or "what this paper really ought to be about is," the teacher rewrites the student's paper in the direction of the teacher's assumptions and interests. Students, predictably, are reduced to resentful acquiescence and one-word answers as their essays and also their thoughts, feelings, and experiences are stolen away from them. Instead of personal revisions students are pushed towards giving teachers what they want. It's clear, too, reading the transcript Carnicelli prints, that both instructor and student are unhappy, even desperate, about how the conference is proceeding because they are both unable to control the roles they have assumed.

Carnicelli recommends a clinical therapeutic model, based on Rogerian techniques, for controlling this little drama of teacher violence. Followers of the psychologist Carl Rogers learn to ask questions that are neither substantive, nor leading, nor even truly interrogatory. Instead, the therapist responds from within the communication in an effort to move it along towards greater clarity in whatever direction the speaker chooses. The guiding rule is not to intrude but instead to allow the speaker to explore levels of awareness below the surface of the familiar discourses that the speaker has learned to employ precisely in order not to go further. The Rogerian therapist exhausts the familiar discourse strategies by prompting the speaker to go further; eventually, the speaker ends up saying what he thinks. While the teacher, in Carnicelli's view, does not aim at a therapeutic exploration, he believes the non-leading response can very well help certain kinds of students make certain kinds of clarifying discoveries about what they want to say.

Carnicelli's observation about our readiness to leap into pauses in our student's halting communication is very important. All teachers feel the pressure of being supposed to possess full expertise on all fronts related to their discipline, and composition presents a special problem since, potentially, it verges on everything. The integrity of the student's own communication must be defended against our readiness to appear to know everything. Indeed, instructors should be using student conferences to help students gain greater command over their communicative intentions and to affirm their authority in their own writing. My students, however, seem to need more than what Carnicelli's important lesson in what not to do can provide. Most of them come to the writing courses with such impoverished notions about English (as they call it) and writing assignments that we rarely get to those delicious moments of self-exploration in a partially-formed essay. The essays they write, especially early in the course, tend not to be real enough to warrant deeper exploration.

Having gone on at such length about the positive value and limitations of certain leading efforts to understand student conferences, I am ready to present my own. The writing problems of most of my students are not to be found in the local events of their essays, nor do their problems, in origin at least, stem from their inability to extend their awareness into deeper levels of what they have written. While I do have some students who are prepared to venture boldly into the complex terrain of what is real for them, most of my students are inhibited by very confused ideas about what writing these papers is even about. For so many of them, an essay assignment is merely a test of spelling and punctuation. In this same group, there are usually also fundamental problems in imagining communication that is not precisely bound by an immediate context. Unless I can find a way to break through these two problems, I believe all the polishing of surface rough spots will make no difference, and the attempt to explore the depths of experience directly will also be futile. I believe, too, that the attack on these problems can only be successful in student conferences.

My first step is to inform my perceptions of my students with as much information as I can gather about the social processes that formed them, processes from which, as a middle-aged professor of English, I am fairly well insulated. My students come from the city that stretches out below my window, from the endless prairies of residential squalor, from the barren shopping-mall communities of the near suburbs—and from the dismal schools that have taught them, if nothing else, that they do not count for much and that writing assignments are another test to prove it. Of course, I have those few students who do not fit this profile and a larger group of students whose problems go so deep I cannot really hope to make much difference; but the great middle do fit my profile and really challenge my wit and tenacity. I find I cannot think of any of them as "the student" but only as members of a gallery of types that, nevertheless, share common problems such as regarding essays as tests in mechanics and failing to be able to work within the conventional communicative context of college writing assignments.

Most of us know that solutions to these problems involve, respectively, getting students to feel like saying something real in their essays and getting them to say it with confidence and in an appropriate way for an appropriate audience. However, effecting these solutions requires very different strategies in conference with different types of students. I choose my conference strategies with reference to social/historical information that I have gathered about my students, and my strategies are aimed at getting them to draw on what is important to them outside the university. Such conferences, while pursuing definite principles, cannot follow set procedures. They are not even bound by the sort of restrictions that begin "one should be careful never to . . . " Thus, in the following example, I make every effort to "get under the skin" of my student so that she will be forced to make a connection between her experience and her writing in school. My example, in some ways extreme, is intended to demonstrate the importance of understanding the social/historical dynamics in a student conference and of employing this understanding to change the student's outlook on writing.

Karen H. lives less than a mile from the university, on a noisy, crowded, deteriorating street of beaten row-homes. She went to a nearly all-black high school where eighty percent of the students score below the sixteenth percentile in standardized tests. She is malnourished and has such poor lower teeth that her speech is badly impaired. She never speaks in class and often seems about to fall asleep. Her writing, including her in-class writing, is clear, but mechanical and uninspired. When I look more closely, I notice that she stays very close to the text she is writing about, paraphrasing at every turn. Her in-class essays are pastiches of what we have read, and virtually word for word. It is easy to conclude that Karen H. is simply a lazy, unimaginative, robotic student.

Nevertheless, her most recent in-class essay shows an impressive ability to recall complex passages from the readings. I consult my student profile card. (I conduct a survey at the beginning of the course to gather information about their educational, work, and leisure experience and especially about their experience with writing outside of school settings.) I discover that Karen H. writes for a neighborhood newssheet. My second guess, therefore, is that she does not know what sort of communication is allowed her in these assignments and that she is overwhelmed by the mannerisms, the size, and the very exalted idea of the university.

I ask Karen H. to see me in conference. Her writing does not show significant or numerous surface errors; her local event problems could be defined as overly mechanical paraphrase; my guess is that a "what do you really mean to say here" approach will not get far since she has made no effort to say anything. The essay was to be about the obedience to authority controversy arising from the readiness of subjects in Stanley Milgram's famous experiment to follow orders that appeared to inflict injury on others. The students had read an account of the experiment and a review that attacked Milgram's conclusions by arguing that this readiness to obey was the bond that made all social processes orderly and dependable. Students were to develop a view on this question using examples out of their own experience. Karen H.'s essay was nothing more than a cautious restatement of the original essays. I decide that the best approach in this conference will be to look out the window with her.

Karen H. arrives five minutes early and waits in my outer office, holding her slight body with narrow intensity. I make a quick decision not to be smiling and reassuring but to disrupt her expectations. When she enters I am looking out the window at "Coketown," and I call her over to tell me what she sees. Caught off guard, she tells me she sees factories. I tell her it is impressive, all those warehouses and quiet streets and the high-rise public housing, and she regards me as if I am crazy but says nothing. I tell her it must be nice living down there amidst all that old quaint architecture (I use words like "amidst" and "quaint"). She nods, looks down at her notebook, and no doubt wonders how much longer this dumb conference will last.

I walk around to the window behind my desk and look down at the local school, a light-industry structure of the 1950's with bars and fencing guarding every way. I tell her how fortunate people in this ghetto neighborhood are to have a modern school building. I see a twitch go through her as, I guess, she remembers the disorder and threat and incompetence and squalor of her school days in that very school or one quite like it. Karen H. begins to reach for her paper folded in her notebook, aware that the twenty minutes are going by and we do not have much time left to talk about her comma splice errors. Breaking another rule of conference technique, I seat her across the room as I sit down at my desk; I decide also that if a phone call comes through, I will answer it and isolate her further.

Karen has every reason to be annoyed. Early in the course, all my students wrote about their neighborhoods, so Karen has the right to expect that I know where she lives. I see she is becoming restless; the time is passing, I am saying stupid things about something she really knows about; I am being rude; I am negating her earlier communication; I am wasting her time; and the comma splices wait there impatiently. She would like to tell me I am wrong about the neighborhood, but she cannot decide exactly in which direction: that the neighborhood is meaner than what my words are saying; that the neighborhood has more interest and dignity than what I probably think.

I take another risk. The paper she brought to talk about is one more piece of ventriloquism, typical of her "do-the-assignment" approach to writing. I read the essay aloud very slowly so its emptiness will reverberate like an empty trash barrel. I ask her whether she thinks it is an interesting essay; she tells me it fulfills the assignment. I ask her who would be interested in reading her essay; she answers that she does not know. (Apparent in her manner is that she has not thought about the question.) In a show of exasperation I ask her whether she has anything to write that would be important for anyone to read—this is an especially offensive remark since Karen H. is a writer in her own neighborhood. As if in a chance way, I wave back at the local school out the window behind me. I ask her whether she could tell me anything about obedience and authority in that school. She tells me, with something of a smirk, that she guesses she could.

I tell her I would really like to read that essay since people who have experienced school like that hardly ever get to write about it. She begins to tell me how it is in those schools, and I listen with evident interest. I offer her praise and encouragement, but I tell her I do not think she will get much out of college until she learns to take advantage of the fact that she comes from a place in society that university people know very little about. In one sense this is a lie, but my aim is to provide her a superior perch, a position of authority that writers need. I ask her to rewrite her essay; hard worker that she is, Karen H. agrees. I ask her whether she has heard of James Baldwin; she has, but has not read anything of his. I suggest she read just the opening few pages of "Sonny's Blues" to help her think about what goes on in city schools. I know very well she will read the whole story and probably the stories that follow it in the anthology, those by Langston Hughes, Ralph Ellison, and Richard Wright. I know that she will probably feel proud because she will have done all that extra work on her own. I lend her the anthology with these stories: this "giving of a gift" is a way to smooth over the annoyance I have put her through; it's a sign of trust and a commitment on my part meant to elicit a feeling of obligation on hers.

I look at my watch and comment that we have no time left. I suggest that she look at the handbook for an explanation of comma splices and ask me about them after next class if she thinks she does not understand. I muster my warmest, most paternal smile and deliver the moral of our twenty-minute drama: "it's having something to say and a reason for saying it and an audience to imagine we must say it to that makes us good writers." I ask her to repeat this rule, which she does perfectly. Karen H. gathers her books, showing special care for the book I have loaned her, and I walk her out of my office, past the secretary's desk, and down the hall to the elevator. I leave her with the mock-admonishing gesture of poking my finger towards her and saying sternly "I want that paper by next Tuesday." I want her to know, if she does not already, that this conference has been made up of a great deal of play-acting.

I have re-enacted this conference, at perhaps tiresome length, as the best way of explaining what is missing in the prevailing efforts to lay down rules about student conferences. "The student" we read about in these essays does not exist, and rules appropriate for "conferencing" this shadow are an illusion. Karen H. represents a special type of student, a type that in my experience requires an extraordinary intervention on my part. This is not to say, however (as my students in their adolescent, democratic fervor love to say), that every individual is entirely different. Each school, in its own setting, with its own special mix of students, has its own gallery of types. It's a crucial part of a teacher's task to master this set of types and to study what social/historical processes produced the variety within the set, which is bound to be great.

Along with Karen H. this semester, there was Hans K., whose father is an English professor, and who wrote highly ornamental, upholstered, Victorian prose. We spent two hilarious sessions making fun of his attempt to emulate the ridiculous idea he had of his father's writing. I taught him to write a young man's "lean and mean" style by mocking his pomposity, and we both had a jolly good laugh about it.

With Ruth J., a woman in her early fifties who had raised six children in hard circumstances, I became a conspirator, the only other adult in the group of youngsters. Like almost all mature students, Ruth J. felt both intimidated by and superior to her much younger classmates. In conference, therefore, I treated her as if she were a co-teacher who, because of her life experience, really did know more about the politics of communication. I taught her by talking about all the things the young people were having trouble figuring out. I asked her advice on how to help them. Ruth J.'s early essays were confused and tentative; however, provided this perch of security, Ruth J. got past her feelings of inadequacy and wrote out of her depth of experience with authority and assurance.

And there is the sly young fellow whose career goals can already be computed in property acquisitions, stock options, and dreams of executive boardroom triumphs. There is the young woman whose father left when she was ten and who has made a small career of punishing herself by not succeeding. There is the middle-class son of the shopping malls, who is hungry for adventures—maybe even the adventures of philosophy and radical social thought and curious art that can give shape to his cynical unease.

After many years of teaching I am beginning to understand the *dramatis personae* of my classes and to have some ideas about how to use student conferences to turn my students toward genuine communication. It is amazing how all aspects of their writing improve when students have a clear sense of self, of purpose, and of audience. I am impressed, too, with how often gaining that sense of clarity is the result of making a connection between those worlds outside my office windows and what the university has to offer. I find that this connection is best made in the dynamic personal setting of these conferences. Translating student conferences into other, simpler paradigms of efficiency, smooth client relations, or psychotherapeutic self-exploration impoverishes education. We can do better than that.

Notes

[1] *A Writer Teaches Writing* (Boston: Houghton Mifflin, 1968).

[2] "One to One: Tutorial Instruction in Freshman Composition," in *New Direction for Community Colleges* (San Francisco: Jossey-Bass 2, 1974), 55-83.

[3] "The Student-Teacher Conference," *College and Composition and Communication,* 28 (December 1977), 338-342.

[4] "The Writing Conference: a One-to-One Conversation," in *Eight Approaches to Teaching Composition,* ed. T. R. Donovan and B. W. McClelland (Urbana, Illinois: NCTE, 1980).

PART III

The Teaching of Grammar

6

Teaching Grammar:

Some Linguistic Predictions

JUSTINE T. STILLINGS and MUFFY E. A. SIEGEL

Justine T. Stillings holds a Ph.D. in linguistics from the University of Massachusetts at Amherst. She has taught writing and linguistics at various levels, published work on theoretical syntax and metrics, and worked as a manager for IBM and as executive vice president of a small computer company. Currently she is teaching linguistics at Tianjin Normal College in the People's Republic of China.

Muffy E. A. Siegel holds a Ph.D. in linguistics from the University of Massachusetts at Amherst. She is currently Director of the Program in Linguistics at Temple University in Philadelphia, as well as a member of the English Department there. She has published articles on syntax, semantics, morphology, and stylistics, and a book on the formal semantics of adjectives, Capturing the Adjective. *She regularly teaches linguistics, composition, and grammar.*

The major contribution of modern transformational linguistics[1] to the teaching of writing lies in its ability to make predictions about the way grammar should be taught. This kind of linguistics has nothing to contribute to teaching paper organization, clear logical argument, creative writing, or even accurate diction. Transformational linguistics does, however, concern itself with the nuts and bolts of grammatical sentences and, thus, can yield information that is useful in the teaching of grammar.

Of course, the rules that tranformational syntacticians come up with can't be used in the classroom directly. We can't, for example, simply take the research on language structure that linguists have done, toss away all of the standard grammar books, give the set of linguistic rules to students, and imagine that their grammar problems will be solved. Some people tried this in the sixties and succeeded mostly in giving linguistics a bad name among English teachers. Of course, it didn't work, because it was like handing someone the laws of Newtonian physics and expecting the person to be able to change a flat tire after reading them. Transformational grammar and Newtonian physics are scientific theories, and a theory is not a set of instructions for operating in the real world. Theories can, however, provide guidelines for predictions about things in the real world. Newtonian mechanics, for instance, predicts that when changing a tire, you are not going to get the lug nuts off if you turn them in the wrong direction. However, it doesn't tell you what tool to use to turn the lug nuts. It predicts that if you set the jack on soft mud and then attempt to jack up the car, the jack will simply sink, but it doesn't tell you how to use a jack or what kind to buy.

Similarly, linguistics is going to come up with a set of predictions about grammatical errors in student compositions, and these predictions can be converted into some real-world guidelines for teachers, but not instructions for students. For instance, theoretical linguists believe that a perfectly systematic linguistic competence underlies our sometimes inconsistent linguistic performance. That is, every speaker has subconsciously internalized a set of language rules for his own dialect, even if he sometimes breaks those rules when actually speaking. This hypothesis allows us to classify student errors in an illuminating way, one that will help in fashioning pedagogical techniques. It predicts, for instance, that students will make errors due both to performance factors and to competence factors. Performance errors should be relatively easy to correct, since the student will recognize them as violating the tacit knowledge of the language that constitutes his linguistic competence. Competence errors, on the other hand, ones that arise from writing according to an internalized set of rules other than those of Standard Written English, will be harder to correct, according to the predictions of our theory, because, for any speaker, his own rules are the correct ones.

These predictions are borne out. Students make both the individual, apparently careless errors due to performance factors and the systematic, consistent ones attributable to competence factors. Figure 1 is a classification of common writing errors according to these theoretical predictions.

Some of this classification may require explanation. The first category of errors, the true careless errors, is hardly worth worrying about. The student can correct them if only he can learn to reread the paper carefully and objectively. Asking him to watch someone else read it or to read it aloud to someone will help. The second type of performance error, though, deserves more comment. These errors come about largely because a student is writing very quickly or very slowly and either omits things in a hurry or loses track of where he has been because his ideas are developing much more quickly than the writing. Students who write slowly, for example, can easily forget what sentence they are in the middle of and begin a new one half-way through, or forget that they haven't written a new subject yet for the new predicate that they've just introduced. An example of this kind of slow writing error is this collapsed sentence from a real student paper, example number 3 in Figure 1:

(1) The paintings by Hogarth were drawn in 1750 are called "Beer Street and Gin Lane" look alike.

Figure 1

Classification of Errors in Standard Written English
(F = finite state rules; D = decidable rules; N = non-decidable rules.)

Examples from Student Papers

Performance Errors	Errors due to temporary factors (fatigue, carelessness)	words left out, inserted recopying mistakes	1 If my feet see they they would have to agree with that. 2 What is really love about Temple University is the Humanities Building.
	Errors due to more permanent factors in writing situation for student (slow writing, fast writing)	D collapsed sentences D non-parallelism N mismatched subject and predicate D subject-verb number agreement D extra commas	3 The two paintings by Hogarth were drawn in 1750 are called "Beer Street and Gin Lane" look alike. 4 The most appropriate thing to do was to sit on a couch and placed a foot in her mouth. 5 The rates of specific taxes are a political process. 6 . . . the soft, chic look of good leather shoes have a tendency to disappear. 7 Facts that are backed up in the book, are backed up by people.
	Errors from not having internalized rules of Standard Spoken English.	D non-standard inflections D be-deletion, other non-standard auxiliary verb structure	8 I was and still is frighten of cats. 9 The sole been repair so much until the new sole laying against the old.
Competence Errors	Errors from not having internalized rules of Written English	F capitalization F spelling F/D punctuation D fragments, run-ons N wordiness N misplaced modifiers N vague pronouns	10 It stood 15 feet from the floor. With confusing wires extended. 11 In the picture were two women, one of them may have been our prof. 12 Unlike the pilgrims, my family they have some different traditions of their own. 13 The citizens' behavior of Flatland . . . 14 There is no evidence that the fruits of this type of society are more bountiful than one where freedom exists.

Lack of parallelism and mismatched subjects and predicates, as shown in the fourth and fifth examples on the chart, arise for similar reasons. There is evidence for the hypothesis that all these errors arise because the students are writing so slowly that they simply forget what they have been doing in between two conjoined phrases or between the subject and predicate. This evidence is simply that students do not generally make these rather bizarre errors in speech, which is more rapid than writing.

Others of the slow writing errors arise a little differently, in that the student who writes slowly applies a rule of grammar, but an incorrect one. Many students who have subject-verb agreement problems, for instance, seem to apply the rule mistakenly to the verb and the noun closest to it, rather than to the noun which is structurally related to the verb as its subject:

(2) The bookcase with the green shelves are heavy.

One can hardly say that the student does not know an agreement rule. The problem is that by the time he has laboriously written the words intervening between subject and predicate, he has lost track of what noun the rule should apply to. Again, as with previous slow writing errors, he would be unlikely to make such an error while speaking. (Apparent number agreement errors in speech are usually a result of dialect differences, which will be dealt with below.)

Many comma errors are related to the slow writing problem as well, and in fact derive from the correct application of a rule English teachers have given to students: insert a comma wherever you would pause. Slow writers pause often as they write. Thus, in the extreme case, they might be well-justified in inserting commas between almost every word. Luckily, the problem is not so severe, but careful application of the comma-for-a-pause rule is likely to result in sentences such as the following (example 7 in Figure 1):

(3) Facts that are backed up in the book, are backed up by people.

Predictably, we do not find this comma error in short sentences, because even the slowest writers would not think of pausing for breath between the subject and verb of sentences like

(4) She, won.

The tricky problem with all these errors is that simple proofreading will not help much. Slow writers are likely to be slow readers as well, so the comma-for-a-pause rule, for instance, is no better when presented as a proofreading tool than when presented as a rule for writing.

The student needs instead reliable, mechanical rules defined in terms of the sentence structure, which does not change according to the rate of writing. Linguistic theory, it turns out, makes some interesting predictions about the best ways to formulate these rules, and we return to those predictions later. It's enough now to note that the subject-verb agreement rule and even comma rules can be formulated structurally so that students will find it possible to use them as proofreading and revision tools:

(5) Find the main noun(s) of the subject noun phrase and the main verb(s) of the predicate. Make them agree in number.

(6) Use a comma
   a. before a conjunction joining two sentences
   b. after an introductory phrases which is not the main noun phrase of the sentence
   c. on both sides of parenthetical phrases
   d. in a series where conjunctions are omitted
   e. in dates and addresses
   f. between a quotation and the words of attribution

Of course, to apply these rules, the students must understand sentence structure. To make sure that they do, we actually teach grammar students to diagram sentences using a highly simplified and pedagogically adapted phrase structure grammar.[2] Students who have a great many grammar problems find that learning to diagram in this way is an extremely worthwhile investment of time. First, a phrase structure grammar shows in a positive way how to generate grammatical sentences (see note 2). In addition, once the student can diagram his own sentences, he knows just where the main noun of the subject is, where the parentheticals are, and so on; so he can apply the rules for grammar and punctuation that his teacher formulates. Using the rules of Standard Written English then is revealed as a learnable skill rather than a matter of inspiration and class background. If the rules are properly formulated, the student can apply them mechanically; he will just go through the checklist of those phrases that require commas, for instance, and put them in.

Precise, mechanical proofreading tools are also required to eliminate the last two types of student error, the competence "errors." However, these rules will have a slightly different status, according to our theoretical framework, since they are meant to allow a student to correct errors which are not errors at all from the student's linguistic point of view. These "errors" are consistent with his internalized rule system, which is not that of Standard Written English. A student's internalized rule system may differ from that of Standard Written English for two different reasons. The student may speak a dialect other than Standard Spoken English, perhaps Urban Black English. As is well-known now, systematic differences in verb and noun inflections and in auxiliary verb structure often carry over into writing from non-Standard spoken dialects.[3] Alternatively (or in addition), the student may simply not have acquired the rules of the writing dialect, which is different from *any* spoken dialect.[4] Students who have trouble with the writing dialect rules may be suffering from the effects of bad grade school teaching, since these rules, if mastered before the age of twelve or so, are not forgotten. If students do not have much active experience with written language until later, though, we can predict that they are likely to have a "foreign accent" in their writing for the rest of their lives, as people who learn second languages as adults often do.[5]

The first few errors involving the rules of the writing dialect—capitalization, spelling, and punctuation—are rather obvious candidates for this category. The last four may look a bit surprising. It may seem strange that sentence fragments and run-ons are considered errors involving use of the orthographic period peculiar to writing and not a more fundamental difficulty in sentence structure. However, the evidence that fragments and run-ons are an orthographic problem comes from the fact that students who use periods incorrectly have no difficulty in speaking grammatically effective sentences, regardless of dialect. They simply can't divide up phrases visually on paper.

The "wordiness" problem may seem an odd one for inclusion as a grammatical error relevant to the writing dialect. However, evidence for this inclusion comes from the tape recordings of spoken Standard English and transcriptions such as the passage below from a "talking piece" by the poet David Antin, which is followed by a more appropriate written version of the same material.

(7) . . . i remember a situation   and this is a
good place to remember this situation because this is the university
of indiana   and the university of indiana is one of the great places
in anthropological linguistics   and this situation i recall   the
writing of a distinguished anthropologist   a man named warner
william warner[6]

(8) I remember a situation described by the distinguished anthropologist William Warner.

Apparently, the ephemeral nature of sounds in the air requires us to use a great deal of repetition in speech for our listeners to be able to follow us, and to introduce new information gradually, as Hindle's paper in this volume explains. The permanent nature of writing, however, with its automatic accessibility to review, makes such techniques purely wasteful. Note, for example, how difficult it is to follow speeches prepared by speakers who are reading their talks from prewritten papers. The information flows by at a rate conventional for written prose, but much too quickly to keep track of when heard aloud unless a listener employs the utmost concentration. It thus appears that "wordiness" can occur when a student uses, in writing, strategies which are appropriate in spoken English.

Two other problems which appear to be related to the writing dialect rules are those of modifier placement and pronoun reference. In spoken English, the connection between modifier and the word modified is greatly affected by intonation. Some kinds of modifiers in spoken sentences can be placed unambiguously almost anywhere as long as the proper intonation changes are made. In writing, the rules for modifier reference are much stricter, and with no availability of intonation or non-linguistic context, seem to rely largely on word order. A modifier must be placed more closely to the phrase it's modifying than to any other possibly ambiguous phrase. Thus sentence (9) will work in speech with a higher and rising intonation on the final phrase, but in writing must be represented as (10):

(9) We saw a flamingo driving through the Everglades.

(10) Driving through the Everglades, we saw a flamingo.

The pronoun reference rules for English are likewise much freer in spoken English than in written English. In written English, it's obligatory that a pronoun refer to some phrase in the text. In spoken English, this rule is relaxed in at least two ways:

1. Due to the availability of gestures, pronouns need not refer to words at all—we can perfectly well point to a tree and say, "That's beautiful." In fact, there's evidence that pronouns in speech do not generally require linguistic antecedents. (See Hindle's paper in this volume.)

2. In spoken English, pronouns can regularly refer not only back to something that was previously mentioned, but ahead to something that is coming up in the conversation. (For instance, "this" in "OK, I've told you what happened first. Now, this is what happened next . . . ") Forward-referring pronouns are rare in writing. ("When she had finished her chores, Cathy fell asleep.")

The importance of isolating the writing dialect rules in this manner is that we often encourage our students, in accordance with an old adage, to "write as you speak," and then criticize them for wordiness and dangling modifiers, both of which follow directly from writing as one speaks.

A technique for teaching students to avoid such competence-based errors is, once again, practically-formulated, structurally-based rules that can be used by students in proofreading sentences to check them mechanically for adherence to the rules of Standard Written English. Since sentences containing competence errors are grammatical according to the students' internalized grammars, if they proofread with the idea of simply looking for errors, they will find very few of the competence errors. Rules must therefore be easy enough to use that the students can measure every sentence by them and even use them as a kind of tool or procedure for translating what they write into Standard Written English.

Often, the linguist's insight into particular aspects of language can aid in the formulation of rules that are practical and intuitively appealing enough for students to be able to come to proofreading with the necessary rules in mind. For instance, students who do not use standard inflections on nouns and verbs often understand the point of adding the required *s*'s and *ed*'s better once they see that all such words are composed of a root word plus a word ending, which gives information about number, person, or tense, even if it's a zero-morph, as in the case of English singular nouns. In addition, the very precision of the linguist's formal versions of grammatical rules can lead us to a more general kind of real-world prediction about the formulation and teaching of grammar rules. Because linguistic rules are so precise that we have been able to construct mathematical proofs about them, they enable us to predict which forms of rules will be hardest to learn so that we can, where possible, avoid formulating such rules and give students as much time and help as possible to learn to use the unavoidable difficult ones.

The main thrust of an important article by P. S. Peters and R. W. Ritchie has nothing to do with teaching grammar.[7] Nevertheless, their work does entail that, while some rules of grammar can be formulated so they are easy enough to memorize and apply in proofreading almost immediately, there are going to be some sentences which it will be impossible to proofread for grammaticality in any mechanical way because of the mathematical properties of the grammatical rules involved. Easy rules to formulate, learn, and use are the finite state ones (marked F on the error chart), which involve simply learning lists of items requiring a particular treatment. The spelling of individual words, hyphenation, and capitalization are usually formulated as finite state rules: The first word of each sentence must be capitalized. If it's not, capitalize it. Words broken at the end of a line must have a hyphen. If they don't, add one. Words must be spelled correctly. Check every word longer than two letters in a dictionary, and if you've made a mistake, correct it.

A little bit harder are the context-free decidable rules (marked D on the chart), which involve identifying classes of structures to which to apply some procedure. Fragments and run-ons, periods, commas, agreement, case, parallelism are, at best, formulated this way. It's necessary to be able to diagram a sentence in order to handle these rules confidently, but once a student can do that, they are as mechanical as the finite state rules: First, make a diagram (perhaps mental) of the sentence. Has it got a main noun phrase and a main verb phrase? If not, add whatever is missing. If you seem to have two of each and no subordinators, put a period in the middle. Does the information in the ending on the subject agree with that in the ending on the verb? If not, then add an *s* to one or the other, and so on. As long as the students can diagram, and the rules are presented with a great deal of practice and many reminders, students should be able to apply them in proofreading after a reasonable time, perhaps a semester.

The hardest rules, ones we must give students the most time for, are the non-decidable rules (marked N on the chart). These, like the context-free decidable rules, apply generally to all sorts of cases. However, they require extremely lengthy mathematical formulations, and there is no mechanical way to make sure that you have applied the rules correctly. Aspects of the language which seem to require this kind of rule are pronoun reference and modifier placement. There's no mechanical error-checking procedure for these rules, largely because proper use of pronouns and placement of modifiers involve avoiding ambiguities arising from other parts of the sentence. But there are a few finite state or context-free decidable tricks that we can teach: Does the paper have the word *this* in its first sentence? If so, change it. Does each pronoun in a paragraph refer back to some specific word or phrase that has been written out completely earlier in the paragraph? If not, then use a noun, not a pronoun.

Mastering techniques for handling aspects of the language that are governed by non-decidable rules requires a long time and a great deal of practice. These aspects are, in an objective, mathematical sense, hard. Moreover, even experienced writers struggle with making pronoun references clear and placing modifiers correctly. Formal linguistic theory, then, makes it possible for us to predict that we will be more successful if we avoid, when possible, formulating non-decidable rules and look for finite state or context-free decidable versions where we can. It will be easier, for instance, for students to identify prepositions if they have a finite state rule for doing so. Yet, a rule common in grammar books is that prepositions are words that show the relationship between a noun phrase and some other word in the sentence. With this definition, students not only have to do syntactic analysis of much of the sentence in order to recognize a preposition, but, because of the vagueness of the definition, they also never know for sure whether or not they have found a real preposition. Most words show a "relationship." The guidelines that emerge from the predictions of transformational and mathematical linguistic theory would lead us to recommend a finite state replacement of the preposition-finding rule, such as a simple list of words that can be prepositions. Once students have learned such a list, a relatively easy task, finding most prepositions will be completely mechanical. The teacher will have more time to spend on those aspects of Standard Written English that are not amenable to finite state formulations.

The traditional teaching of grammar in composition classes has been out of favor for a while. Teachers and students know that people do not learn to write by studying grammar. Unfortunately, people do not learn to produce sentences that conform to the grammar of Standard Written English merely by writing, either. A reasonable solution to this standoff would seem to be to recognize revision as a central activity of writing and to provide students with precise, easy-to-use revision tools for grammar. Work with grammar, then, *is* work with writing, since grammar rules are revision tools, and revision is at the heart of being a writer.

In order for students to use such tools successfully, they must have an accurate, but not necessarily complete, knowledge of the structure of English, and they must have tools that are formulated and presented in the most appropriate way. We have not covered enough linguistics here to present a coherent and realistic picture of the structure of English and of the character of linguistic methodology. We have described instead the great variety that exists both in the origins of grammatical errors and in the properties of the rules meant to help students correct them. We have shown why it is, for instance, much more difficult to correct a competence-based error than a performance one or to use a non-decidable rule rather than a finite state one. We hope that such considerations will help guide the formulation and presentation of more and more grammar rules with which students can write.

Notes

[1] We mean by "modern transformational linguistics" research in the tradition first developed most notably by Noam Chomsky.

[2] A phrase structure grammar consists of rewrite rules which specify the possible constituents of each phrase and their order. These rules are meant to represent explicitly the tacit knowledge that speakers have of the hierarchical organization and linear order of their language. Phrase structure grammars can be used to generate phrase structure diagrams (called "trees") of particular sentences, which show how those sentences fulfill the requirements of English sentencehood by "following" the phrase structure rules, that is, by matching a tree generated by those rules. Below is a very simple fragment of a phrase structure grammar for English and one of the infinite number of trees generated by it. (S = Sentence, NP = Noun Phrase, VP = Verb Phrase, PP = Prepositional Phrase Art = Article, Adj = Adjective. Constituents in parentheses are optional parts of the phrase whose name appears on the left of the arrow.)

```
S   ⟶  NP   VP
NP  ⟶  (Art) (Adj) N (PP)
VP  ⟶  V (NP) (NP) (Adj) (PP)
PP  ⟶  P    NP
```

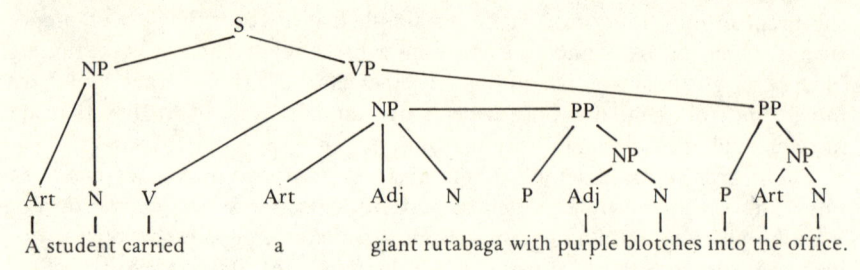

```
                        S
        NP                          VP
                              NP            PP          PP
                                                  NP          NP
Art  N   V      Art      Adj   N      P   Adj   N    P   Art   N
 |   |   |       |        |    |      |    |    |    |    |    |
 A student carried a    giant rutabaga with purple blotches into the office.
```

Students in a grammar course, naturally, can develop a more complete set of rules which allows them to produce trees that illuminate the structure of even the most complex English sentences.

[3] See, for instance, William Labov's "The Study of Nonstandard English," National Council of Teachers of English, Champaign, IL, 1970.

[4] See, for instance, Anthony Kroch's and Donald Hindle's papers in this book, or Andee Rubin, "A Theoretical Taxonomy of the Differences Between Oral and Written Language," Technical Report No. 35 (Cambridge, MA: Bolt, Beranek and Newman, 1978).

[5] Such a prediction would be based on the widely accepted theory that there is a critical period for native language acquisition (See Eric Lenneberg, *Biological Foundations of Language* [New York: John Wiley and Sons, 1967]) and that part of mastering written language is analogous to learning a new language or dialect.

[6] David Antin, *Talking at the Boundaries* (New York: New Directions, 1976), p. 61.

[7] P. S. Peters and R. W. Ritchie, "On the Generative Power of Transformational Grammars," *Information Sciences*, 6 (1973), 49-83.

7

Discourse Organization in Speech and Writing

DONALD HINDLE

Donald Hindle received his Ph.D. in linguistics from the University of Pennsylvania in 1979. He has worked as a researcher on a project on the social motivation and interactional use of sound change in the Philadelphia speech community and on other quantitative studies of linguistic variation. A freelance linguist, he is currently consulting on several projects, including one at Bell Labs developing a new approach to parsing natural language syntax.

I'm going to talk about some of the specific rules that organize what we say and what we write, how the rules differ in speech and writing,[1] and some implications of these differences for the teaching of writing. But first I want to make my basic assumptions clear. The central assumption that underlies what I'll say, and in fact the central assumption that makes the scientific study of language possible, is that everyone's use of language is "rule governed." That is to say, no matter how chaotic a person's speech may seem, it is invariably the case that if we take time to look carefully and deeply at what is going on, regular patterns emerge. Behavior that at first glance seemed aimless, or simply wrong, turns out to be highly structured and tightly controlled. Accordingly, spoken language, even speech of the most horribly incorrect sort, is governed by rules in exactly the same way that written language is governed by rules. Unlike the rules for writing, which are mostly conscious and are learned through schooling, the rules of speech are for the most part unconscious and are learned outside of school. For this reason, it's often difficult to recognize that we are following rules when we are speaking, and specific linguistic studies are necessary to discover them.

I take it as a given that, before even beginning to learn to write, everyone has assimilated a rich and complex set of unconscious rules to govern speech. There are rules of grammar, rules of word choice, rules of politeness, rules for organizing what is said, and rules for all the many other subparts that make up language. Here, I'm going to focus on the rules that are used to organize what is said, and I will show that they seem to be the underlying source for many of the grammatical differences between speech and writing.

Differences in the grammars of speech and writing are caused by differences in the way they organize what is said. The importance of this finding is clear: if people are to learn to use the correct grammar for writing, they must learn the appropriate rules for organizing written discourse. Furthermore, since spoken language has its own rules for organizing discourse, learning to write cannot be considered simply learning additional rules for writing. Rather, it must involve replacing some of the rules for spoken language with rules for written language. Thus, it seems likely, as I will argue later on, that learning to write means not only learning new rules, but also learning to give up some of the rules for organizing discourse that work perfectly well for speech.

After discussing in general what discourse rules are like, I will describe three broad differences in how discourse is organized in speech and writing. For each difference, I will give examples and evidence from a carefully matched sample of student speech and writing. Finally, I will discuss briefly one sample paragraph of the writing of a college composition student to illustrate the influence of spoken discourse rules in the syntactic choices of inexperienced writers.

The Power of Discourse Rules

The rules that organize discourse are for the most part invisible, but nevertheless they are quite powerful. A couple of examples should make it clear how important they are. One easy way to see the importance of discourse rules is to look at people who haven't yet learned the rules: young children. There's a period in the course of learning to talk when children tell stories that are, for adults, bizarre. Consider the following example:

Mother: What did you do at the party?
Child: He pulled a rabbit out and it ran down and Charles had to go home.

The problem is not that the child has forgotten what happened, for it's easy to get the full picture by asking the right questions. Nor is it that the child is lacking the grammatical resources for telling the story. Indeed, young children sometimes use quite complicated syntax, while the grammatical structures typical of narratives are for the most part chosen from among the simpler forms. Nor is the problem that the child can't keep the story in mind long enough. Even very short stories can count as stories and children routinely produce much longer inept narratives.[2] Rather, the problem appears to be that the child simply does not know how to tell a story. A knowledge of what happened (the facts) and of how to make sentences (the grammar) is not enough; the child must also learn how to make a story that other people recognize as coherent: how to introduce background, what can be referred to, how much must be said and what can be left out. In short, he or she must learn the rules for organizing the discourse of stories.

A second example of the power of discourse rules comes from Charlotte Linde's study of how people describe the layouts of their apartments.[3] It's easy to imagine several ways to describe an apartment layout. You could describe the layout as if you were looking down from above; that is, you could draw a verbal map. Or you could describe each step on a route through the apartment, starting at the front door and proceeding through the rooms. Either of these approaches would succeed equally well, and most people guess that we should be free to choose either type of description. But, in fact, the two types are far from equally likely. Linde found that people almost universally describe the layout in terms of a tour; the map type description virtually never occurs. Moreover, within the tour type of description, there are additional rules that constrain the details of what can be said, so that the syntax of these descriptions is, within a narrow range, highly predictable. It's clear that such a high level of predictability can only be the result of a tightly constraining set of underlying rules. But the rules are not rules of the grammar. Rather, they are rules for organizing what is said. The point is that we can't say or write anything without following some rules for organizing discourse.

The Discourse Model

The first question to ask about the rules that organize discourse in speech and writing is: what is organized? Put another way: what is language about? The answer is, of course, much too complex to even begin to explore here. But one aspect of discourse organization is clear. We talk about things. In stories, there are people; in the description of an apartment layout, there are rooms; in arguments, there are positions and beliefs and facts. I will call these various things that we talk about *entities*.[4] One of the jobs we must accomplish in any discourse is to introduce the relevant entities, and to keep the entities straight. (In talking about what is going on in discourse, I will rely on two terms: *text* and *discourse model*. I will use *text* to mean any stretch of speech or writing—the actual language used. I will use *discourse model* to mean the interpretation associated with a text—in short, what is talked about.) If we look at talking or writing as processes, then they involve the step-by-step production of a text. And as the text itself is produced, a corresponding discourse model is gradually built up. Entities are introduced and referred to, propositions relating them are expressed, attention is shifted from one focus to another. Obviously, the discourse model is not the same as the linguistic material that I'm calling the text. But it's also important to recognize that it isn't the same as the physical material of the world. Conceptually, the discourse model must be viewed as a semantic structure that is associated with the text by the process of *discourse interpretation*.

Discourse interpretation, associating a particular discourse model with a particular text, is a complicated process. When people communicate through a linguistic text, either by speech or writing, everyone involved must individually construct his or her own version of the discourse model underlying it, and the hearer or reader must construct a similar discourse model to associate with the same text. This is done on the basis of the text itself, together with general knowledge about the world. In one sense, a text can be seen as "a set of instructions from a speaker to a hearer on how to construct a particular discourse model."[5] In general, the different models that are constructed are so similar that participants can act as though they share the same model.[6]

Of course, the problem of constructing the appropriate discourse model is not the same in speech and writing. Spoken communication typically relies to some extent on specific background knowledge that is shared by the participants but is not available to the general population. Speakers assume that their audience will use this knowledge to construct the correct discourse model. If the audience does not in fact have the necessary background knowledge that the speaker assumes, there will be a problem in communication: the audience will be unable to construct the proper discourse model. But in speech, because the participants are in the same place at the same time, instantaneous adjustments can be made for any mismatch of background knowledge. Conversational partners are in fact always reassuring each other, both by verbal and nonverbal means, that they are talking about the same model. Every speaker of the language makes constant use of a detailed knowledge of the verbal and nonverbal signals that are used to affirm a shared understanding. In writing, the problem of a mismatch in background knowledge is considerably more severe, because the writer and the reader can't reassure each other that they have the same model. If a writer wrongly assumes that his readers have some background knowledge that they in fact lack, there will be a problem of communication, and it will not be corrected. But gauging exactly what knowledge to assume is not easy, and beginning writers commonly make the mistake of assuming too much knowledge on the part of their readers.

To investigate the rules for organizing discourse, we thought it would be useful to compare samples of speech and writing in which the difference in background knowledge is minimized. The sample for the study we did is a matched set of spoken and written texts from a group of college-level beginning composition students. Each student was tape-recorded during a sociolinguistic interview designed to elicit spontaneous speech on several topics, including narratives, argumentation, and description.[7] Because the interviewer was a university professor and the interview took place on campus, the speech is necessarily fairly formal. The level of the background knowledge assumed by the students is at a minimum, since this was the first meeting with the interviewer. Later, each student wrote a series of compositions on the same topics that were covered in the interviews, and it is these samples of speech and writing, matched for topics, that I will be talking about. Because the students were inexperienced writers, their writing shows many of the features of speech that better writers avoid. But despite these similarities, there are striking differences in the way the spoken and written discourses are organized.

Referring in Speech and Writing

One of the main things that people do when they talk or write is to refer to the things they are talking about. Referring to things is, somewhat surprisingly, no simple matter. Consider the following sentence:

(1) I met the director and he couldn't tell me where his office was.

Here, there is a noun phrase "the director" and this refers to some entity in the discourse model, call it The Director. (We don't really know much about the discourse entity The Director except that it is presumably a person in charge of something. That doesn't matter. The important point is that there's a noun phrase in the text and an entity in the discourse model associated with the noun phrase.) But what happens when you come to the word "he" in this text? There are two ways to look at what happens. On the one hand, you could say the pronoun "he" refers to the noun phrase "the director." This would mean that reference is a relationship from one *linguistic element in the text* to another *linguistic element in the text*. On the other hand, you might say that the pronoun "he" refers not to an item in the text at all, but rather to the *discourse entity* which I am symbolizing as The Director, just as the noun phrase "the director" refers to the discourse entity The Director. Under the first view, reference is considered to be a relation between one element of the text and a second element which is also in the text—I'll call this *text-to-text* reference. According to the second view, reference is seen as a relation between an element of the text (a noun phrase or a pronoun) on the one hand, and an entity in the discourse model on the other—*text-to-discourse-model* reference. In both ways of looking at reference, the noun phrase "the director" can be said to refer to an entity in the discourse model. The difference arises for subsequent references. In the text-to-text view, subsequent noun phrases, such as "he" do not refer to the discourse model; rather they refer back to the previous noun phrase in the text. In contrast, the discourse model view holds that "he" and all subsequent noun phrases are just like the initial noun phrase and refer directly to elements in the discourse model. No link to other elements in the text is established.

Now, it turns out that these two ways of looking at reference correspond to the difference between spoken and written reference. That is: *Speech views all reference as text-to-discourse-model links; writing demands that text-to-text links be established.* This difference in referential strategy has a wide range of consequences in the syntax of speech and writing. First, it allows spoken discourse to refer to items in the discourse model that are not yet in the text. Thus, sentences like

(2) She went to the tanning studio three extra times and *it* still wasn't very dark.

and (in a discussion of abortion)

(3) Just because mitosis occurs doesn't mean *it*'s a person.

are common in spoken discourse, but are prohibited in writing. In sentence (2) the italicized *it* refers to *a tan*, and in sentence (3) the italicized *it* refers to *the fetus*. I want to emphasize that the problem with these sentences is not that they are hard to understand. Figuring out the meaning of the italicized pronouns is no problem, because the things referred to are already in the discourse model. Nevertheless, in spite of its understandability, this type of pronoun reference is not proper for written discourse. To see why, it's necessary to consider reference in a little more detail.

One of the most important questions in organizing a discourse is the question of whether an entity is *new* to the discourse.[8] Corresponding to the two ways of looking at reference, there are two ways of looking at newness: 1) Is the entity new to the text? That is, has there been a noun phrase referring to it already? 2) Is the entity new to the discourse model structure? That is, has the construction of the discourse model involved this entity (regardless of whether it has been referred to before)? Of course, if the referring noun phrase is old in the text, it must necessarily be old in the discourse. Prince calls these *evoked* entities. If on the other hand, the referring noun phrase is new to the text, it may be either new to the discourse model, in which case Prince calls it *brand new,* or it may be implied by the discourse model—what Prince calls *inferable*.[9] This classification is summarized as follows:

	New in Text	New in Discourse Model
NEW	+	+
INFERABLE	+	−
EVOKED	−	−

In sentence (1) above, the noun phrase "the director" refers to a *new* entity, "he" refers to an *evoked* entity, and "office" refers to an *inferable* entity.

Now when a pronoun is used to refer to an *inferable* entity, as in examples (2) and (3) above, no text-to-text connection can be made, since there is no previous item in the text for the pronoun to refer to. This means that when pronouns are used in writing to refer to *inferable* entities, the reference rule for written discourse is violated. And in fact, the rate of pronoun use for *inferable* entities in speech is more than three times the rate in writing. Table 1 shows this comparison on the basis of the student sample.

	Spoken	*Written*
Pronoun	59 (20%)	13 (6%)
Total NP	299	224

Table 1. Inferable entities: use of pronouns in spoken and written texts by five college composition students.[10]

The text-to-text constraint on reference in writing has implications for more complex types of noun phrases as well. Sometimes, a noun phrase referring to an *inferable* entity can contain within it a second noun phrase that refers to some other entity. For example, in the sentence

(4) The table fell on its side.

the noun phrase "its side" has as head the noun "side." This entity is in turn *inferable* from the second noun phrase "its," which refers to the *evoked* entity "table," appealing to the general fact that tables have sides. The possessive pronoun "its" acts as an *anchor,* connecting "side" to the table. Thus, this type of noun phrase is called *anchored inferable.* Consider the difference between (5) and (6)

(5) We were walking across the compound when I saw the commander.
(6) We were walking across the compound when I saw the commander of our unit.

In sentence (5), the *inferable* entity, "the commander," is tied to the subject "we" only because the discourse model thus far constructed refers to a military base where "we" refers to soldiers. In sentence (6), the *anchored inferable*, "the commander of our unit," is additionally tied by the noun phrase, "our unit," to the antecedent "we." This additional tie to the text helps to satisfy the text-to-text constraint on reference in writing, and therefore *anchored inferables* are preferred in writing.

Table 2 shows that in the student sample, *anchored inferables* of this sort are twice as common in writing as they are in speech.

	Spoken	*Written*
Anchored Inferables	74 (2%)	91 (4%)
Other Noun Phrases	3621	2368

Table 2. Anchored Inferables in spoken and written texts by five college composition students.

The difference in *inferables* between writing and speech extends to the choice of modifiers in noun phrases. Noun phrases can have modifiers both before the head noun (premodifiers) and after the head noun (postmodifiers). Modifiers before the noun tend to be used for making predications. They are typically adjectives, as "the blue car," or "the central question," but even when premodifiers are nouns, they act as predicates rather than referring to a specific entity in the discourse model. For example, consider the premodifier "air" in "air hammer." Postmodifiers, on the other hand, are typically clauses, reduced clauses, or prepositional phrases, each containing a noun phrase. Typically this noun phrase refers to an entity in the model—that is, it is an anchor. Examples of postmodified noun phrases, with the anchor italicized, are:

(7) the man who dropped off *the package*
(8) the book outlining *that strategy*
(9) a friend of *my lawyer's*

Because of the anchoring function of postmodifiers (which establishes a text-to-text connection), they are relatively more frequent for *inferable* entities in writing than in speech. Table 3 shows that the probability of postmodifiers for *inferables* in writing is twice that in speech.[11] (There is no significant difference in the probabilities of postmodifiers for *new* or *evoked* entities.)

	Premodification		*Postmodification*	
	Spoken	*Written*	*Spoken*	*Written*
New	.22	.30	.30	.33
Inferable	.15	.32	.08	.16
Evoked	.07	.19	.08	.10

Table 3. Probabilities of pre- and post-modification for *new, inferable,* and *evoked* entities in spoken and written discourse of five students.

For premodification, the typical slot of predications, Table 3 shows that *inferables* behave just like *new* entities in writing, but are intermediate between *new* and *evoked* in the spoken sample. For postmodification on the other hand, *inferables* are intermediate between *new* and *evoked* in the writing, but behave just like *evoked* entities in speech. This clearly shows that speech tends to treat *inferables* more like *evoked* entities, while writing treats them more like *new* entities. This difference is exactly what is expected from the difference in reference between speech and writing. *Inferables* are like *new* entities as far as not having been mentioned in the text goes, and thus written discourse, which demands text-to-text links, treats *inferables* like *new entities*. But *inferables* are like *evoked* entities as far as the links to the discourse model are concerned, and thus speech treats *inferable* and *evoked* entities alike.

The higher rate of postmodification of *inferables* in the written discourse obviously means that these noun phrases are syntactically more complex than in speech. However, this difference between the two channels in the rate of postmodification is the consequence of a difference in referential strategy. Thus, this channel-based difference in syntactic complexity is not the consequence of different grammars, but of different rules of discourse organization which constrain coreference. It's worth emphasizing that in this case an obvious way to teach novice writers to produce the more complex syntactic structures typical of speech would be to emphasize the necessity of making text-to-text referential connections.

Finally, the difference in referential strategies in speech and writing affects the use of sequences or *chains* of pronouns in which each pronoun refers to the same entity. In particular, the length of such chains is limited in writing but not in speech. Table 4 shows the distributions of pronoun chains for the speech of an upper class Philadelphian recorded in a sociolinguistic interview, and for the texts of three articles from popular newsmagazines.

Length of Chain	*Speech*	*Writing*
1	33	44
2	16	16
3	7	10
4	8	5
5	1	2
6-10	3	0
10-20	3	0
20+	1	0
mean length	4.0	2.7
median length	2.2	1.9

Table 4. Chains of coreferential third-person pronouns in spoken and written discourse.

Two influences apparently operate on pronoun chains—one which is shared by both speech and writing, and one which differentiates the two channels. Both channels show a strong tendency to favor short pronoun chains. Probably this is because most of the entities which are referred to by third-person pronouns come into focus for only a short time, and are therefore referred to (whether by noun or pronoun) only a few times. But the second tendency strikingly evident in Table 4 is that no pronoun chain as long as six occurs in the written sample, while in speech the chains may be arbitrarily long. The longest stretches for 32 pronouns with no intervening coreferential noun, while the longest written chain is 5. I would argue that the constraint in written discourse demanding a connection between a pronoun and an antecedent noun in the text means that long pronoun chains present a problem for the resolution of reference. No such problem arises in spoken discourse, however, since it does not have the text-to-text constraint.

It's interesting that the prohibition of long sequences of pronouns in written discourse *has* to be stated in terms of the pronoun form in the chain of noun phrases; it can't be stated only in terms of the discourse relationship. But this type of text sensitivity is precisely what the text-to-text reference constraint demands. A similar sort of text-sensitivity in written discourse is found in the constraint which prohibits repeated use of the identical noun phrase to refer to the same entity. It is a well-known and often overused prescriptive rule of writing that the writer should vary the words used to refer to the same entity. In speech, which is not sensitive to the text in the same way, such a constraint cannot even be stated, and so repetitions of the identical noun phrase are frequent and natural in our interviews. The following sentence,

(10) I went through *law school*, and got my degree from *law school*. When I graduated from *law school* . . .

would be excluded from written discourse.

Introducing New Information in Speech and Writing

A second problem in organizing discourse is how to introduce new entities into the text in the first place. A speaker or writer has to decide when and where to introduce new entities, and the choice is constrained by specific discourse rules. Spoken discourse has a general constraint on introducing new information, namely: *In speech, new information is introduced one piece at a time.* The obvious corollary of this constraint is that new entities are introduced one at a time. I should be a little more specific about what I mean by "one at a time." The most natural interpretation of this is "one sentence at a time," but we have to be a little careful about the meaning of "sentence." In writing, sentences are marked by punctuation, while in speech, intonation serves a similar function. However, the systems of punctuation and intonation don't correspond precisely. I will define "sentence" in syntactic terms so that speech and writing will be comparable. I will take "sentence" to mean one main clause with all its associated subordinate clauses. This means coordinated clauses are treated as two sentences. Using this definition, it's possible to compare the introduction of new information in speech and writing.

Certain syntactic devices are preferred in speech because they satisfy the one-new-piece-of-information-at-a-time constraint by introducing *new* entities while adding a minimum of other new information. Clauses that satisfy this constraint can be called *introducer clauses*. Among the introducer clasuses are four types:

1. existential *there* clauses, such as, "There's a store on the corner."
2. *have* clauses, in which the direct object of the relatively empty verb *have* is a *new* entity and the subject is old: for example, "He had a *new* Chrysler."

Discourse Organization in Speech and Writing 81

3. locative phrases, in which a *new* entity is introduced as the location of an entity already present in the discourse model: for example, "I was sitting on *a table.*"
4. noun phrase fragments, in which a *new* noun phrase constitutes an entire information unit: for example, "*This guy.* I once knew this guy."

Table 5 shows that each of these clause types for introducing *new* entities is more common in the sample of speech than in writing.

Introducer	*Spoken*	*Written*
there	14	7
have	9	3
locative	11	5
NP fragment	7	1
Total	41	16
with other new information	19	35

Table 5. Syntactic structures for introducing *new* entities

In Table 5, the four syntactic structures for introducing *new* entities can be contrasted with another type of clause which both introduces a *new* entity and contains other new information. Such clauses include cases where the *new* entity is the subject of the clause, the direct object of an action verb, or another complement of a verb. As Table 5 shows, this more complex way of introducing *new* entities is more common in the written sample than in speech.

Empty Subjects in Speech

In addition to the constraint on the amount of new information per unit, speech also imposes the following constraint on where the new information can occur: *In speech, subjects should be empty.* By this I mean that grammatical subjects should contain as little information as possible. Subjects such as expletive "there" and "it" contain no information at all, and the pronouns "I" and "you" contain very little. At the other extreme, noun phrases referring to *new* entities contain a lot of new information. For this reason, spoken discourse has relatively fewer *new* entities than written. Table 6 shows the relative percentages of *new* entities in speech and writing of our student sample for grammatical subjects, direct objects, and predicate nominals. Two patterns are evident in this table. First, in each of the grammatical positions, relatively fewer *new* entities occur in speech than in the writing. This is apparently a consequence of the limitation on the amount of new information: since only one entity in a sentence can be new in speech, the

	Spoken			Written		
	New	Total	% New	New	Total	% New
SUB	76	1358	(6)	87	704	(12)
DO	191	419	(46)	155	283	(55)
PN	92	117	(79)	71	86	(83)

Table 6. New entities in spoken and written texts of five composition students: subject, direct objects, and predicate nominal.

number of *new* entities is reduced. Secondly, the size of the difference between speech and writing depends on the grammatical function. Predicate nominal position, a favorite place for introducing *new* entities in speech, shows the least difference between speech and writing. Direct object position, which includes both the verb *have*, which is used for introducing *new* entities, and other transitive verbs which are not favored for introducing *new* entities, is intermediate. In subject position, which is a heavily disfavored position for introducing *new* entities in speech, there are fully twice as many *new* entities in writing as in speech.

I indicated above that spoken discourse has more expletive "there" subjects than written, and this is one way of making the subject empty. Another syntactic technique used in spoken discourse to empty the grammatical subject is to put empty pronouns in subject position. By empty pronouns I mean those that refer to the speaker or the listener ("I" and "you" and their variants), the pronouns "you" and "they" when they refer to generalized entities, as in sentences (11) and (12), and the pronoun "it" in its nonreferential use as in sentence (13).

(11) You never know!
(12) They wrecked the school system.
(13) It's ridiculous that he said that.

In the spoken sample, well over half of the grammatical subjects (739/1358) are this sort of empty pronoun, while in the writing, only about a third of the subjects are of this type (243/704).

In addition to these perfectly grammatical constructions that are preferred in speech, the spoken grammar contains syntactic constructions that are absolutely prohibited in writing, but work to allow sentences to obey the same constraint on new information. Sentences (14) and (15) are examples of a sentence type that is prohibited in written discourse but occurs repeatedly and productively (although rarely) in speech. Michael Montgomery reports this type of construction, which he calls "fused sentences," in a variety of levels of speech, from informal conversation to television interviews.[1,2]

(14) That's all they used to do was fight.
(15) It's a real problem is what it is.

A first guess might suggest that these are syntactic "blends," which result from inattention or carelessness. Of course such blends do occur, but this sort of construction obeys highly specific constraints and occurs regularly and productively; therefore it should not be viewed as just an error. Consider the special syntactic features of this form. The following conditions must apply:

1. The middle noun phrase plays two roles. It is predicate nominal with respect to the first *be* and subject with respect to the second *be*.
2. Both verbs are forms of the verb *be*. (Sentences like, "He found a book lay on the shelf," do not occur with any regularity.)
3. The three noun phrases are coreferential.
4. The first noun phrase is an empty form.
5. The second noun phrase is complex.
6. The construction occurs as a single intonational unit.

These constraints on the construction clearly accomplish its discourse function. The first noun phrase and the first verb in these constructions are empty, convey no information, but they succeed in obeying the discourse constraint by presenting a sentence with one new piece of information and a subject position that is empty.

A Sample Composition

The following composition from the student sample illustrates the intrusion of the discourse rules of speech into a written composition. I have separated the composition into sentences as I defined them above (ignoring the punctuation) and have assigned a letter to each sentence to facilitate reference.

a. One time . . . there was a group of kids hanging out . . .
b. What happen was two cars pulled up
c. and a couple of guys and girls got out . . .
d. All of a sudden I see a guy run full speed to one of the cars.
e. He pulled out a bat and started running after one of the other guys.
f. The story was that the guy was trying to take his girl home . . .
g. Her boyfriend found out
h. and that's when he ran for the bat.
i. After he got the bat he ran to get the kid that was with his girlfriend.
j. He caught up to him
k. and it happen to be in the middle of the street.
l. The kid swung the bat
m. and the other kid hit the floor.
n. The bat just missed his head.
o. His head would of no longer been on his shoulders.
p. It really looked like a duel.

q. But only one guy had the sword.
r. He swung the bat three more times
s. and the other kid missed all three by a hair,
t. no more than that.
u. A couple of guys stopped the kid with bat
v. and I believe it was just in time because he was ready to kill the other guy
w. After that not one of the kids were allowed in the club.

It's clear that this composition has many problems, and they come from a variety of sources. What's striking is how many of the problems are simply the result of the inappropriate use of the discourse rules of speech by this novice writer. Consider some of the criticisms we might make.

1. Pronoun reference is confused. This is true only if you try to establish text-to-text links. In fact, the meanings of all the pronouns are deducible from the meaning of the story.

2. Too many sentences are short and repetitive. If the writer is trying to fulfill the spoken discourse constraint that one piece of new information be presented per sentence, then the choices of syntactic form are severely limited. Even if the writer knows many different syntactic constructions, he must be freed from the spoken language constraint before he can use them.

3. The grammatical subjects are uninteresting and repetitive. But this is exactly what spoken discourse demands.

Look in detail at sentences j. and k. The first problem is that there are two pronouns "he" and "him," and several nouns to which they might refer. But in terms of the discourse model, the reference of these pronouns is unequivocal. If "he" caught up with "him," the "he" must refer to the person who was running after someone (mentioned in the preceding sentence), and "him" must be the person who was being chased. No other interpretation of the reference of "he" and "him" makes any sense. The fact that the reference of these pronouns can't be resolved in terms of the previous nouns in the text is no problem for spoken discourse, and thus the writer of this composition did not recognize the problem. A second problem is that the writer has used two sentences when a single sentence would have been sufficient. Why did the writer use an entire separate sentence to say that the meeting happened in the middle of the street? The answer is clearly that otherwise there would be two new pieces of information in the sentence. And notice that the second sentence has a completely empty "it" for subject. Throughout the composition, new entities are introduced in their own sentences, one at a time.

Overall then, the noun phrases in this composition make sense in terms of the story, even though the pronouns often seem to point to the wrong antecedent noun phrase in the text. The sentences have one new piece of information per sentence and the subjects are low information items. In short, this writer has made the mistake of applying the rules of spoken discourse in writing, and the resulting composition doesn't work.

Summary

I have argued that whenever a person says or writes anything, he or she is following powerful, unwritten rules which organize the discourse. The problem confronting an inexperienced writer is that writing organizes discourse using different rules from the ones that he or she has used perfectly well for speech. In particular,

1. Written discourse demands that for all referring expressions, the reader must be able to locate an antecedent in the text. Spoken discourse has no such constraint.
2. Spoken discourse limits the amount of new information in each sentence.
3. Spoken discourse favors relatively empty noun phrases as grammatical subject.

The task facing a new writer is not only to learn to apply the rules for written discourse, but to learn *not* to apply the rules of spoken discourse. The mistakes made by new writers can often be traced to the fact that they have not yet assimilated the special rules of written discourse, but that, as experienced speakers of the language, they know all too well the rules for organizing spoken discourse.

Notes

[1] This work was supported by the National Institute of Education Grant no. G78-0169. Anthony Kroch was the principal investigator and was a great help to me in the work I talk about here.

[2] Harvey Sacks, "On the Analyzability of Stories by Children," in *Directions in Sociolinguistics,* eds. John Gumperz and Dell Hymes (New York: Holt, Rinehart and Winston, 1972), 325-345.

[3] *The Linguistic Encoding of Spatial Information,* Diss. Columbia University, 1974.

[4] Recent work in the field of discourse analysis has converged on the general mode of discourse structure that is the basis of this analysis: Barbara Grosz, "Focusing in Dialog," SPI International. Technical Note No. 151, July 1977; Bonnie L. Webber, *A Formal Approach to Discourse Anaphora* (New York: Garland Press, 1979); Ellen F. Prince, "Toward a Taxonomy of Given-New Information," in *Radical Pragmatics,* ed. Peter Cole (New York: Academic Press, 1981), 223-255. Prince is the source of the specific analytic model and terminology I use here.

[5] Prince, p. 235.

[6] Grosz, 1977.

[7] The interviews were of the type designed by Labov (William Labov, *The Social Stratification of English in New York City* [Washington: Center for Applied Linguistics,

1966])aimed at eliciting unself-conscious speech. Anthony Kroch conducted the interviews with 18 members of Jim Hessinger's composition class at Temple University in the spring of 1979. My discussion is based on a subsample of this data.

[8] The distinction between *new* entities and *given* ones is well established in the literature of discourse analysis and has been specifically invoked in a variety of studies (M. A. K. Halliday, "Notes on Transitivity and Theme in English. Part 2," *Journal of Linguistics*, 3[1967], 199-244; Susumu Kuno, "Functional Sentence Perspective," *Linguistic Inquiry*, 3[1973], 269-320; Judith Weiner and William Labov, "Constraints on the Agentless Passive," *Journal of Linguistics*, forthcoming, 1983). As commonplace as the distinction is, however, the cases where given or new status is obvious are a minority, and intermediate cases abound. This is also the finding of Prince (1981), who introduces a series of distinctions to elaborate and specify the intuitive concepts of given and new. The following discussion is presented in terms of the distinctions she draws.

[9] For the present discussion, I exclude from consideration those *new* entities which are what Prince calls *unused*—essentially, unique entities. Nor will I consider *evoked* entities which are *situationally evoked*, that is, cases of exophoric reference.

[10] The differences between the spoken and written samples that I point out in Tables 1, 2, 5, and 6 are significant by chi-square test at the .05 level.

[11] The probabilities in this table are derived from a variety grammar of noun phrase syntax in this sample (Donald Hindle, "A Probabilistic Grammar of Noun Phrases in Spoken and Written English," in *Variation Omnibus*, eds. D. Sankoff and H. Cedergren [Edmonton, Alberta: Linguistic Research, Inc., 1981], 369-378).

[12] Michael Montgomery, "The Syntax and Rhetoric of Fused Sentences in English," NWAVE-X, Philadelphia, 1981.

8

Syntactic Interference from the Spoken Language in the Prose of Unskilled Writers

ANTHONY S. KROCH

Anthony S. Kroch holds a Ph.D. in linguistics from the Massachusetts Institute of Technology. He is now a member of the Linguistics Department of the University of Pennsylvania and the principal investigator of an NIE grant, "A Quantitative Study of the Syntax of Speech and Writing." He has published extensively on the topic of class and grammar, as well as in semantics and quantitative linguistics.

Introduction

That every normal child learns to speak the language of his or her community is at once a truism and a fundamental axiom of linguistics. In order to speak the community's language the child must learn the grammar of this language, the system of rules that defines the set of possible sentences. It is on the basis of these rules that speakers produce utterances adapted to their communicative and expressive purposes by choosing among grammatical possibilities. The more we study speech, the more impressed we become with the skill of the ordinary native speaker in manipulating the rules of grammar for communicative purposes. Yet, after years of development and practice with the spoken language, this same native speaker, when writing, all too often produces sentences that are halting or garbled, even leaving aside the frequent incoherence of the discourse.

For a linguist, the difficulty that people have with the syntax of written English is surprising. Although there are grammatical differences between spoken and written forms, they are minor from the point of view of the system as a whole. A writer whose only fault was failing to follow the grammatical conventions of the standard written language would be guilty of nothing more than occasional errors, easily corrected in revision. Indeed, the research with college composition students that I will be discussing suggests that they have learned to avoid such faults; only the very least proficient college-age writers seem to make frequent grammatical errors.[1] Why then is the syntax of apprentice writers so often limited and awkward, even when it contains no overt errors or nonstandard usage? I think that interference from speech-derived constraints on syntactic organization is in part responsible and that freeing writers from the dominance of these constraints should be a major task of writing pedagogy.

These constraints on the syntax of speech derive from the conditions under which speech is produced and interpreted. The spontaneous utterances of daily life, the most characteristic use of spoken language, are produced under severe time and memory constraints, which limit the amount of syntactic planning that speakers can allocate to each sentence.[2]

In order to maintain fluency, speakers must plan sentences at roughly the same rate that they utter them and, when sentences are long, must begin uttering them before they are completely formed.[3] The requirement that spoken sentences be syntactically planned in "real time" is paralleled by a corresponding constraint on sentence interpretation. As the words of a sentence are perceived and recognized, they must be fitted into a syntactic and semantic analysis on the basis of which the sentence is interpreted. Again this analysis must proceed at as fast a rate as words are transmitted. Any slower rate would soon lead to an intolerable accumulation of syntactically unanalyzed strings of words in memory.[4]

The real time constraint on sentence production and interpretation must have an effect on the syntactic complexity of the sentences that speakers use in spontaneous spoken language.[5] However, we would expect this effect to be much mitigated in written prose. After all, the writer is not constrained to form sentences in real time or to put them on paper before they are fully formed. Similarly, the reader can read as slowly as need be to grasp the syntactic form of the sentence. Further weakening the time constraint on the written language are the possibilities for the writer of revising and for the reader of re-reading difficult passages.

There is as yet no proof in the research literature that the difference in syntactic complexity and other syntactic differences between writing and speech are the effect of differences in the time and memory constraints on processing for the two channels. Certainly this effect cannot explain all differences. Some are clearly consequences of the important differences in discourse organization between writing and speech (see the paper by Donald Hindle in this volume). When we looked in detail in our research at two or three differences in syntactic usage, however, we found common threads linking the cases whose only plausible explanation seemed to have to do with the kind of processing constraints I have been describing. If we accept this conclusion provisionally, we can perhaps draw a lesson for how the process of learning to write might be influenced by these processing effects. Due to the conditioning of a lifetime of speaking, unskilled writers will continue to some extent to obey in their writing the constraints on syntactic form that speech imposes. The result will be an impoverished writing style. An important part of learning how to write will then be learning to relax speech-derived constraints on syntactic organization to make full use of the syntactic resources of the language. The relaxation of these constraints will make available a wider choice of syntactic forms and levels of complexity. Apprentice writers will then have to learn two things: first, to use a wider range of syntactic alternatives and second, to make their syntactic choices serve expressive and communicative purposes.

This idea of what apprentice writers have to learn about the syntax of written prose contrasts with the commonly held view that learning to use written syntax is a matter of learning "grammar," the correct use of constructions that are often distorted in speech. Under this view, writers must obey a stricter set of rules than speakers, who, depending on circumstances, are free to alter word order and collapse syntactic distinctions in a way that obscures meaning but facilitates utterance. No doubt such cases exist; they are listed at length in any guide to usage. Still, the strictest adherence to the rules governing such cases will hardly produce a mature prose style, and too much concern for them will more likely produce writer's block than effective prose. If we are correct in our hypothesis, apprentice writers need help in learning to recognize and exploit the freedom the written channel affords before, and to a greater extent than, they need instruction in the conventions of written usage. The latter is largely a matter of appearances and superficial style, which can be corrected in revision. The former is a more fundamental matter which influences and perhaps even determines the range of syntactic forms that the writer can exploit to express meaning.

In the following discussion I will try to make a case for our thesis that unskilled writing reflects the apprentice writer's continued dominance by psycholinguistic constraints appropriate to speech. I will present data from speech and writing on the comparative usage and grammar of one common construction central to English syntax, the relative clause. In analyzing the distribution and form of relative clauses in speech and writing, I will demonstrate that the differences we find are most plausibly explicable as resulting from psycholinguistic effects, and that by a number of syntactic criteria, unskilled writing falls between skilled writing and speech in its statistical profile.

The data

My findings were derived from a study of the writing and speech of a group of 18 students at Temple University.[6] The students were a group of working class and lower middle class white[7] Philadelphians of both sexes between the ages of 19 and 23 who shared the same linguistic dialect. At the time of the study, the spring semester of 1979, they were enrolled in the University's entry level, non-remedial English composition course, Comp. 50.[8] To obtain samples of the students' speech I interviewed each of them individually and privately for about 90 minutes, using interview questions adapted from the schedule developed by William Labov for his study of the Philadelphia speech community.[9] After the interviews, samples of writing on the interview topics were obtained from in-class assignments. By tailoring the contents of the essays to the interviews, we were able to lessen the distortion that content differences between writing and speech samples might have imparted to our comparisons.

A word or two about the methods used in the interviews is perhaps in order here to better indicate what sort of speech we were able to elicit. A Labov-style sociolinguistic interview is designed to approximate a natural conversation and thereby to minimize the linguistic distortion that frequently occurs in the interview situation. Of course, such interviews do not consistently show the relaxed speech typical of ordinary conversation, but the interviewer plans his interventions and questions with the aim of approaching the style of spontaneous conversation as much as possible. The topics are themselves designed to favor relaxed speech because they encourage the person interviewed to draw on personal experience. Because of the interview method used, we were able to elicit fluent and lively conversation from almost all of the student subjects. Nevertheless, the circumstances of the interview—it was conducted on the university campus by an interviewer with faculty status—guarantee that the speech obtained is close to the most formal that these students ever use. This result is appropriate, however, to the purpose of the research, which is to contrast speech and writing. Whatever differences we find between the students' speech and their writing can not be due in any simple way to mere style shifting between formal and informal situations.

Because the matched spoken and written texts so closely approximate each other, we would be likely, if we relied on this sample alone, to underestimate the differences between speech and writing. In one respect, this is an advantage, for we can have greater confidence in the differences that we do find. However, to achieve a broader view encompassing the full range of differences between spoken and written syntax, we must expand our view. One particular limitation of the student sample is that it gives no view of the effects of knowledge of the standard language or of social class differentiation. It is clear that social class differences can have far-reaching effects. Of particular interest, from both a theoretical and a pedagogical viewpoint, is the question of how close spoken and written syntax are in different social groups. Anecdotal evidence suggests that the influence of the written standard on the speech of classes that habitually use written language may be quite large, but that for other classes, spoken syntax differs greatly from the written standard.

To sample the dimension of standard versus nonstandard language, the student material was supplemented with sociolinguistic interviews of professional class and working class white adults and with writing from newspapers and magazines. The professional class adults were four prominent lawyers and businessmen whom I had interviewed in conjunction with a previous research project.[10] The professional class interviews provide a sample of the most standard speech used in the community. The differences between the speech of this group and skilled writing can be assumed to be due to real channel differences rather than to dialect differences between the standard and the nonstandard languages. The data on working class speech consists of four interviews with people from downtown ethnic neighborhoods done by a linguist for William Labov's research project on Linguistic Change and Variation.[11] The interviews were conducted with the aim of eliciting the most relaxed and vernacular style possible. They can be taken as reasonably representative of the working class vernacular of Philadelphia. The grammar and style of this speech are as far removed from the standard language as can be found in the white population and represent the everyday speech environment of the Temple University students in the sample, who are overwhelmingly city raised and working class or lower middle class in origin. It is, of course, true that the population of Philadelphia is exposed to and uses a great variety of speech styles. Therefore, we would not claim that anyone in our sample is limited to the style and dialect that appear on the interview tapes. We do believe, however, that any linguistic influence from speech in the writing of the students is likely to come from the vernacular of daily life and that influence of the written language on speech is most likely to manifest itself in the speech of professionals, for whom writing expository prose is an everyday occupational necessity.

Our source of skilled writing, which we use to provide comparisons with our data, is arbitrarily chosen articles from three Philadelphia daily newspapers, the *Philadelphia Bulletin, The Philadelphia Inquirer,* and the *Philadelphia Daily News,* and from *The New York Times.* These newspapers though written for different audiences, all use exclusively the standard written language, the target language for the apprentice writer. We chose newspapers rather than other printed matter to represent this target because they are aimed at a general audience without special knowledge of the topics under discussion and because their style is straightforward and unornamental.

The results

Relative clauses in speech and writing

In English, as in many languages, the relative clause is a crucial grammatical device. If functions most commonly as a modifier of nouns; that is, it expresses a property of the noun phrase to which it is adjoined. Within its general role as a modifier, which it shares with adjectives and post-nominal prepositional phrases, its semantic function varies according to whether it is restrictive or non-restrictive. The restrictive relative, illustrated in (1) below, helps to delimit the referent of the noun phrase in which it occurs:

(1) The people in this room are all from Illinois. But only the woman to whom John is speaking is from Springfield.

Here the phrase "the woman" is not sufficient to define the referent to which the predicate "is from Springfield" is to be applied, and the relative clause "to whom John is speaking" serves to restrict the reference of the noun phrase to the particular individual of whom the sentence makes its predication. Non-restrictive relatives, on the other hand, do not participate in determining the reference of the noun phrases which they modify. The reference of a noun phrase modified by a non-restrictive relative clause is fully determined by its other modifiers: the non-restrictive relative is merely an appositive commentary that supplies optional added information about the referent. Non-restrictive relatives have a parenthetical intonation in speech, and in writing they are generally set off by commas. Thus, "the woman" in (2) below must be the only woman in the room for the sentence to make sense:

(2) When Bill entered, he noticed that the woman, who was wearing a hat, wanted to leave the room.

The fact that the woman was wearing a hat is added information which could have been left out without impairing the hearer's ability to determine of whom the predication "wanted to leave the room" is being made.

The frequency of restrictive and non-restrictive relatives

Written sentences are on average more complex syntactically than spoken ones, and relative clauses add complexity to sentences in which they occur by adding a level of embedding. Consequently, it is not surprising to find that relative clauses are more common in writing than in speech. Table 1 shows the frequency with which relative clauses are encountered in the samples.

Data Source	*Relative Clauses per 100 main clauses*	*Number of Sentences*
Newspaper writing	29	1042
Student writing	17	2568
Professional speech	14	4127
Student speech	5	10725
Working class speech	3	10645

Table 1. Frequency of relative clauses per 100 main clauses.

The writing/speech difference is evident in these figures, but more striking are two other facts revealed in the table: first, the student writing sample contains many fewer relative clauses than the newspaper sample does and, second, the speech of our professional group contains many more relative clauses than do other speech samples. In consequence, the student writing sample and the professional speech sample look similar statistically, and this grouping of data will appear again and again in various results. It demonstrates that the constraints on syntactic usage characteristic of writing and speech can be effective outside the channel in which they find their most characteristic expression. Thus, professional class speakers, because they have more intimate contact than others with the written language, are more practiced in the psycholinguistic planning that complex syntax requires, and the habit of using complex syntax feeling spills over into their conversation. Indeed, such people can sometimes be said, with justice, to "talk like a book." Conversely, the students, because they are less practiced in using the complex syntax of writing than are the people who write for newspapers, show an influence in their prose from speech-derived constraints. The result is that student writing and professional class speech tend to converge on measures of syntactic complexity.

Just the relative frequency of relative clauses in different kinds of speech and writing supports our basic hypothesis about the nature of unskilled writing, but more evidence can be brought to bear. Consider, for instance, the comparative distribution of restrictive and non-restrictive relatives. These two types of relative clauses are not equally essential to discourse; only restrictives provide information necessary to the determination of reference. Indeed, non-restrictive relatives can always be paraphrased by independent clauses. Because non-restrictives are less essential to expression, we would expect to find a larger difference between speech and writing in the number of non-restrictives than in the number of restrictives. As Table 2 shows, this expectation is borne out:

Data Source	% Non-restrictive	Total Relative Clauses
Newspapers	.33	407
Student writing	.22	434
Professional speech	.28	562
Student speech	.13	483
Working class speech	.11	330

Table 2. Frequency of non-restrictive relatives as a fraction of the total number of relative clauses.

The difference between speech and writing in the frequency of non-restrictives is very large, and within the speech category the differences among the different groups are also very large. Once again the standard speakers show a pattern more like the written language and the working class vernacular speakers show the greatest difference from writing. As expected, the writing of the students is intermediate between skilled prose and vernacular speech, again demonstrating the influence of speech-derived constraints on unskilled writing.

It's interesting to note the effect of genre differences on the relative frequency of restrictive and non-restrictive relatives. As Table 3 below indicates, the absolute frequency of relative clauses is heavily influenced by genre. Relative clauses are more frequent in descriptive writing and argumentation than in narration, and this difference holds both for speech and writing. In newspaper writing, relatives are also more common in news stories than in opinion columns.

Data Source	*Argument*	*Description*	*Narration*
Student writing	19	23	14
Student speech	5	7	2
	Opinion	*News*	
Newspapers	20	39	

Table 3. Frequency of relative clauses per 100 sentences by genre.

If we now consider the data in Table 4, however, we see that the relative frequency of restrictives and non-restrictives in the student data, while affected by the speech/writing dimension, shows almost no genre effects. By comparison, there is a notable difference between news story and opinion in the comparative frequency of restrictives and non-restrictives in the newspaper data.

Data Source	*Argument*	*Description*	*Narration*
Student writing	.25	.23	.23
Student speech	.10	.19	.13
	Opinion	*News*	
Newspaper Writing	.22	.45	

Table 4. Percent of non-restrictive relatives by genre.

This difference reflects a general tendency for the opinion columns to show distributions closer to the speech data than do the news stories. The fact that the newspaper data show a genre difference between news stories and opinion columns is not surprising. The tone of the opinion columns is more conversational and less impersonal than that of the news stories. By the same token, the relative weakness of genre differentiation in the student writing is perhaps a reflex of the writers' relative lack of skill. Where they use speech-like style, they do so not because it is appropriate to their writing task, but because they have not yet fully mastered the usage conventions of impersonal expository prose. The fact that there is a general difference between student writing in the expected direction shows that the learners know in what direction the target language lies, even if its subtleties still escape them.

To further demonstrate that our student writing sample shows interference from constraints that originate in speech, let us now consider an additional and more complex effect on the distribution of relative clauses. Table 5 displays the frequency of relative clauses in subjects of main clauses:

Data Source	Restrictive	Non-restrictive
Newspaper writing	.16	.29
Student writing	.26	.08
Professional speech	.13	.09
Student speech	.19	.02
Working class speech	.12	.00

Table 5. Frequency of relatives on a main clause subject as a fraction of the total number of relative clauses.

In this data we see than non-restrictive relatives in speech tend not to occur on the subject noun phrase, but restrictive relatives occur freely in this position. In other words, a sentence like (3) is particularly unlikely to occur in speech compared to one like (4):

(3) The director, who never came on time, was even early yesterday.
(4) I get mad at John, who always arrives at the last minute.

In contrast, newspaper writing shows a healthy percentage of both restrictive and non-restrictive relatives in main clause subject position. The explanation for the speech data is almost certainly that the appearance of non-restrictive relatives complicates the establishment of the basic subject-verb relations from which both sentence interpretation and sentence generation seem to proceed. There are in English a number of grammatical processes which simplify subject position in order to make it easier to establish the subject-verb relation. Non-restrictive relatives, being entirely optional, are not surprisingly disfavored when they come between the subject and the verb. Again not surprisingly, this effect is much weaker for restrictive relatives, which may be necessary to establish what the subject noun phrase refers to. Once again we see that in the newspaper writing this speech-based effect disappears, because the complexity of computation disfavored by the rapidity of speech processing and generation is not a problem for the slower and less linear processes of writing and reading. Yet—and this is important—the student writing disfavors the occurrence of non-restrictive relatives in subject position almost as much as does the student speech. In other words, the student writers are not taking advantage of the greater syntactic freedom that writing allows in the placement of non-restrictive clauses.

Prepositional relatives

The discussion thus far has been aimed at demonstrating that unskilled writers do not use the full syntactic resources of their language because they are hampered by psycholinguistic constraints carried over through habit from their speech. I have also said that for college level writers, lack of grammatical knowledge is not a major source of writing problems. The import of these claims can perhaps be clarified by contrasting the usage pattern presented in the previous section with a case, as it happens also involving the relative clause, where grammatical knowledge is at issue. To do this, however, we must consider data from less skilled writers than those in our primary sample.

Because Temple University, the source of the student sample, is a large urban school that provides access to higher education for the broadest sections of the Philadelphia population, many students matriculate there whose exposure to and command of standard language is quite limited. To serve this population, the University requires entering students to take a writing placement exam, and it provides remedial courses in composition and grammar for those who fail it. Since our basic student sample was drawn from people who had passed the exam and were taking the standard freshman level English composition course, we might expect to find more problems with the grammar of the standard language among those students placed into remedial courses. For the grammatical item we wish to discuss, the prepositional relative, this is indeed the case. Students in the remedial courses make frequent errors in using the construction.[12]

The construction we shall be analyzing, the prepositional or "pied-piped"[13] relative, is illustrated in (5):

(5) a. the woman about whom we spoke
b. the day on which we chose our course

Such relative clauses are extremely rare in speech and seem entirely absent from the vernacular, where the preposition would appear inside the relative clause in the position of an ordinary complement rather than governing an introductory relative pronoun. The vernacular form is illustrated in (6):

(6) the picture that I was looking at

The fact that pied-piped relatives do not occur in the spoken vernacular raises the question of whether the vernacular grammar provides for them. It is perfectly possible that pied-piping is a grammatical option in the vernacular and that its non-occurrence is due to stylistic or other usage effects. However, extremely unskilled writers make errors in constructing pied-piped relatives when they attempt to use them in prose, which tells us that the prepositional relative poses a truly grammatical problem for some speakers of the vernacular.

In the sample of pied-piped relatives obtained from remedial composition students (see note 12), there were indeed a substantial number of errors. Out of 191 pied-piped relatives in the sample, 74, or 39%, were ungrammatical according to the rules of standard written English, and an examination of the ungrammatical cases can show the nature of the grammatical problem that pied-piped relatives pose for those who do not control their use.[14] Among the nonstandard cases, the most interesting and common error was the use of a wrong preposition in the *wh*-phrase that introduces the relative clause, as in the following examples:

(7) a. College should be a tool in (with) which you dig down into your psyche for an insight into your individual nature.
 b. There was one time in (at) which Patton's personality didn't get him into trouble.
 c. I have discovered many things about western civilization to (of) which I was unaware.

In 23 out of 37 cases (62%) this error involved substitution of *in* for the correct preposition. This suggests that nonstandard pied-piping is grammatically very different from the pied-piping in standard written English. The latter generalizes the rule that forms relative clauses, which links a relative pronoun to a position in a subordinate clause, to allow linking of prepositional phrases that include a relative pronoun. Nonstandard pied-piping, on the other hand, seems to be best described as the use of a generalized oblique relativizer *in which* for any case where the gap position in the relative clause is a prepositional phrase. In standard language pied-piping, the lexical preposition that appears at the front of the relative is either selected by the verb to which it serves as a complement, as in (5a), or is determined by the syntactic and semantic role of the prepositional phrase as a sentential modifier, as in (5b). In nonstandard pied-piping, on the other hand, the preposition is a fixed form, *in*, regardless of the role of the prepositional phrase in the relative clause. Where variation occurs, it seems random, as the preposition that appears has no relation to the syntactic or semantic requirements of the lower clause.

If we now look at the overall distribution in the remedial essays of pied-piped relatives that *would* be acceptable in standard written English, we can discover the source and grammatical nature of nonstandard pied-piping. The relevant facts are given in Table 6:

| | Preposition | |
Source of pied-piped PP	*in*	other
Complement	17	19
Adverb	46	16

Table 6. Distribution of pied-piping acceptable in standard written English.

In this table we see, first of all, that the most common correctly used pied-piped relative clause is one where the phrase *in which* appears and where it functions as an adverb in the relative clause rather than as a complement to the main verb. The following are examples of this usage:

(8) a. another area in which my high school has helped me
  b. neighborhoods in which bands would be activated

Note that in both the examples above, it's possible to substitute the single *wh-* word *where* for the pied-piped *in which*. In the vernacular, the use of *where* in such cases is obligatory, as the pied-piped variant does not occur. Indeed, the use of *where* as a generalized oblique relativizer is a characteristic of vernacular English. The following examples illustrate the broad range of circumstances under which *where* occurs as a relative marker in the vernacular:

(9) We had no welfare or any place where you could go and get any kind of assistance.

(10) a. It's a version of hide-and-seek where everyone goes out and hides and you have to hit them with a flashlight.
  b. It was a situation where we had no choice.

(11) a. [It's] a day where they can eat all their stomach can hold.
  b. It's a time allowed on television where shows are shown that will be enjoyed by the whole family.
  c. Have you ever had a dream where you're falling?
  d. There are always things coming up where I have to use my own judgment.

These examples show that *where* has a broader range of functions in the vernacular than it does in either standard written English or in the colloquial speech of people whose language is strongly influenced by the written standard. In standard written English the relative pronoun *where* is used primarily when the relativized position in the relative clause is a locative prepositional phrase, as in (9). In spoken, and occasionally in written standard language, the use of *where* is broader, extending, perhaps metaphorically, to cases like those in (10). The rule for colloquial standard speech seems to be that *where* can be used in any non-locative environment that in standard written English would take a pied-piped relative with *in which*, suggesting that the *where* relative is a less formal substitute for the pied-piped construction. Only in the vernacular, however, do examples like those in (11) occur.

Since the range of circumstances under which the vernacular allows *where* relatives is broader than the standard allows, we can account for the distribution of nonstandard pied-piped relatives quite simply if we take them to be attempts by the vernacular speakers who do not control the standard grammar of pied-piping to replace the relativizer *where* by *in which*, a form that they correctly take to be its stylistic alternant and wrongly assume to be its grammatical equivalent. Whenever the vernacular use of *where* is the same as the colloquial standard, the substitution of *in which*, the most common form, will produce a string that is acceptable standard written English usage. When the vernacular use of *where* is more extended than the standard allows, the substitution of *in which* will produce a nonstandard result. The employment of prepositions other than *in* will produce further nonstandard results; the prepositions will not be chosen according to the environment of the relative clause since the pied-piped *wh-* phrase is not analyzed as being selected by it. If this account is correct, then nonstandard pied-piping must reflect an attempt by unskilled writers with limited knowledge of standard written English to imitate a standard form whose grammar they do not know. Since no pied-piped relatives occur in spoken vernacular English, we must assume that nonstandard pied-piping is not a normal grammatical feature of that language variety. Rather it is a learner's form like the ones characteristic of second language acquisition. Such forms arise when people aim at a target surface form before they have learned the grammatical analysis that underlies it.[15] The relative regularity of nonstandard pied-piping is due to the writers' reinterpretation of pied-piping with *in which* as a lexical variant of the vernacular *where* relative. The irregular, apparently random, use of prepositions in nonstandard pied-piping must be an attempt to closely imitate in the surface string the variety of prepositions that occur in standard English pied-piped relatives.

It is clear that the implications for pedagogy of our analysis of nonstandard pied-piped relatives differ from the implications of the other results. In the earlier discussion I showed that unskilled writers tend to use relative clauses in their prose in a way similar to the way relatives are used in speech. Nonetheless, the grammar of the relative clause did not appear to differ in speech and writing, and the differences between the two channels were only statistical tendencies. In the case of pied-piped relatives, however, we must draw very different conclusions. The fact that some very unskilled writers use pied-piping in a nonstandard way in their prose demonstrates that they do not know the grammatical rule for forming a pied-piped relative, even though they recognize the form as appropriate to expository writing. To use the form correctly, they must learn the rule that governs it. Here grammatical instruction may be helpful and appropriate. It is important to recognize, however, two qualifications of this tentative conclusion. First, only the most unskilled writers, probably those with the least contact with the written language, give any clear indication that they lack grammatical knowledge of the written standard; and second, it is not clear that instruction is a better way to increase grammatical knowledge than is increased reading of standard language prose. It is, for instance, not at all clear that people who do know how to used pied-piped relatives learned their grammar through formal instruction rather than through reading. At least, however, it is possible in the case of pied-piping to say exactly what the unskilled writer does not know and, when appropriate, to tell him or her how to do it right.

Concluding remarks

I have given evidence that unskilled college-level writers use impoverished syntax in their prose, not because they are ignorant of the rules of the grammar of written English but because they continue to obey in writing constraints on syntactic complexity that arise out of the exigencies of real-time speech processing. Once apprentice writers know the rules of grammar of the standard language, their next step in becoming competent in formulating written sentences must be to suppress certain habits learned in speech that limit syntactic complexity and flexibility. It cannot be easy to learn to expand the range of syntactic possibilities considered in formulating a sentence and to choose among them in accordance with semantic and discourse requirements. Furthermore, the research does not tell us much about how this learning can be facilitated and was not designed to do so. Still, it may be appropriate to look for some small pedagogical indications in the results obtained. Thus it is clear that unskilled college writers need an alternative to the speech they hear and produce as a model for syntactic organization when they write. For some reason, they have not found (or perhaps looked for) such a model in their earlier experience, and without one, their syntax cannot improve, for it will remain hostage to their speech-based habits. The only plausible source for this alternative model is the prose they read. It is perhaps too obvious to mention that developing skill in writing depends on wide experience in reading, but this truism is easily enough forgotten in the compartmentalization of instruction characteristic of the university environment. No writing pedagogy can succeed in developing a fluent style in students who read little and reluctantly.

Reading provides information about the expanded range of possibilities that written syntax exploits and so provides a crucial ingredient in transforming unskilled into skilled writers. Another, and complementary, ingredient in learning to write is developing the use of more complex syntax into a more or less automatic habit so that it can be used fluently and be made to serve expressive purposes. It is striking that the speech of the professional class sample shows so much similarity to writing on all the statistical measures. This result indicates how very important habit is in determining the syntactic organization of a person's discourse: once the habit of using a certain syntax becomes ingrained, it affects all modes of language use. Because habit is involved in writing as much as, if not more than, knowledge, the ability to write well can only come through long and continual practice. This conclusion is hardly novel, but it merits emphasis in a world where so many people manage to avoid writing tasks. The changing of habits is generally a painful process, and if students are not made to confront the difficulty in a sustained way, a competent prose style will remain beyond them. The other side of this story, of course, is that the habit of writing well, once acquired, is a permanent addition to the students' repertoire of skills.

Notes

[1] The sample of student writers from which we draw this conclusion and most of the other results reported in this paper were members of a standard freshman level composition class. Students still ignorant of the grammatical conventions of written English, are, of course, more frequent in remedial classes and in earlier grades.

[2] Kathryn J. Bock, "Toward a Cognitive Psychology of Syntax: Information Processing Contributions to Sentence Formulation," *Psychological Review,* 89 No. 1 (1982), 1-46.

[3] David MacDonald, "Natural Language Production as a Process of Decision Making Under Constraint," MIT Artificial Intelligence Laboratory Technical Report, 1980.

[4] Lyn Frazier, "On Comprehending Sentences: Syntactic Parsing Strategies," (Diss., University of Connecticut, 1979).

[5] F. Boldman-Eisler and M. Cohen, "Is N, P, and PN Difficulty a Valid Criterion of Transformational Operations?" *Journal of Verbal Learning and Verbal Behavior,* 9 (1970), 161-166.

[6] The work reported here represents some of the results of a research project on the difference between speech and writing funded by the National Institute of Education under grant number G78-0169. The final report under this grant is available from the author upon request.

[7] We have limited our sample to white speakers in order to limit the scope of our study. Work which extends our results to include the effect of Black English features on the writing of black apprentice writers is clearly desirable, and would be necessary before any of our conclusions could be extended to cover that situation. It would not be surprising if many of our conclusions were to carry over to Black English since Black English, like nonstandard White English, is a spoken vernacular. Black English is, however, much further removed in its grammar from the standard written language than is the white nonstandard vernacular, so that the separation of dialect-based from channel-based differences is a much more substantial task in the Black English case. This task will hopefully be facilitated by our work on the white speech community, both as presented here and in results we hope to derive in the future. Where the black and white vernaculars show similar differences from the standard written language, we will, of course, have better reason to conclude that channel-based differences are involved.

Where the black and white vernaculars behave differently, on the other hand, we will have grounds to suspect that dialect differences are the cause.

[8] Participation in the project was strictly voluntary for the students, and two of the members of the class chose not to participate.

[9] William Labov, "Field Methods Used by the Project on Linguistic Change and Variation," Texas Working Papers in Sociolinguistics, 1981.

[10] Anthony Kroch, "Dialect and Style in the Speech of the Upper Class," final report to the NIMH for grant MH-05536, 1976.

[11] We are indebted to the interviewer, Ann Bower, for the extremely high quality of these interviews and to William Labov for allowing us access to them.

[12] This circumstance was brought to our attention by two instructors in the remedial program whose professional training and research interests are in linguistics, Professor Muffy Siegel of the Temple University English Department and Ms. Elizabeth Dayton, a part-time instructor in the remedial writing program. In order to study the nature of nonstandard prepositional relatives, we obtained a sample of both standard and nonstandard cases from Professor Siegel, who searched both remedial compositions written

for her and some from Temple files. We also obtained a second sample from the file kept by the Temple writing program with the help of Frank Sullivan, a teacher and administrator in that program. Our debt to these colleagues, not only for access to data but also for crucial suggestions as to its proper analysis, is great.

[13] When a relative clause or question is introduced by a prepositional phrase rather than by a simple *wh-* pronoun, linguists have come to call it (after John Robert Ross, "Constraints on Variables in Syntax," Diss., MIT, 1967) a "pied-piped" relative or question because the pronoun takes with it the governing preposition when it moves to the front of the clause.

Pied-piping can front phrases of any complexity containing a *wh-* word; for example, consider these examples from Ross:

(i) These are the reports which the government prescribes the height of the lettering on the covers of.

As the reader can verify, any level of prepositional phrase or NP can be fronted in (i). With maximal pied-piping we get (ii):

(ii) These are the reports the height of the lettering on the covers of which the government prescribes.

Cases in which more than a simple prepositional phrase is carried along are encountered too rarely in the material to be investigated.

[14] Most of the phenomena in this section were pointed out to us by Siegel and Dayton. Professor Michael Montgomery of the University of South Carolina has made similar observations on the basis of his experience with remedial composition students at Memphis State University (personal communication). Our analysis of the data draws heavily on suggestions made to us by Professor Siegel.

[15] Norbert Dittmar, "The Acquisition of German Syntax by Foreign Workers," in *Linguistic Variation: Models and Methods,* ed. D. Sankoff, (New York: Academic Press, 1978), pp. 1-22.

PART IV

Audience

9

On Writing in the Real World

HAROLD van B. CLEVELAND

Harold van B. Cleveland is Vice President for International Economics at Citibank, New York. He received a B.A. degree from Harvard College in 1938 and a J.D. degree from the Harvard Law School in 1942. He was formerly associated with the U. S. Department of State, with the Committee for Economic Development as Assistant Director of Research, and with the John Hancock Mutual Life Insurance Company in Boston, as Counsel. Before joining Citibank in 1966, he was Director of Atlantic Policy Studies of the Council on Foreign Relations, New York. He is the author of three books and a number of monographs and articles on legal, economic, and banking problems.

To write about writing in the real world, one must first make clear where the real world is and what is different or special about writing in it. My real world is the big organization, a business corporation, government department, labor union or what have you. In other words, a bureaucracy. Here are a few thoughts accumulated over the years about writing in and for the organization. The best of them is from Strunk and White, and it applies to writing generally: "When you say something, make sure you have said it. The chances of your having said it are only fair."[1]

Life in a bureaucracy is something we all know a lot about. One of its defining characteristics is that everyone plays a specialized role. The role is impersonal, in the sense that it engages only a small part of the person's self, though it may take a lot of his or her time. What matters about the organization man is not the things that make him an individual, a whole person, but those that qualify him for a relatively narrow role—a role that someone with a very different self might also play. In short, he is a cog—a large cog, perhaps, but still a cog.

The cogs mesh, or at least they're supposed to. Therefore, a lot of communication is necessary, within the machine and with its external environment, which consists in large part of other bureaucracies. Some models of organization theory picture the business organization as an information factory—a mechanism for buying, transforming and selling information. Writing is therefore a big part of bureaucratic life. The spoken word is fugitive and normally imprecise. To keep the machine running well, the cogs must mesh precisely and continuously. The written word with its quality of persistence through time and its possibility of precision is the lifeblood of organization.

I fancy that the invention of writing in the ancient world went hand in hand with the early development of religious and military organization. Writing may have been unnecessary to preserve a body of myths and legends or to practice warfare of a simple kind. But once the religious and military organizations characteristic of civilized society emerged, more was needed than memory and the spoken word. With their internal division of labor, their complex hierarchies, their rules and regulations, organizations need words of unquestioned lineage and unquestionable authority. When organization emerges, there is too much to remember and too great a possibility of disruptive disagreement to rely solely on an oral tradition. Sacred writ and military instruction are probably the beginnings of true writing.

Be that as it may, writing in and for the organization today has two requirements: impersonality and precision or clarity. Personal style, individuality, emotive quality may distract the reader and impair the main function: to communicate a message that is precise and readily understood. In short, writing in the organization is functional—a means to an end, not an end in itself. The end is the smooth functioning of the machine, but it is more—or less—than that. For an organization is not really or only a machine. It is also a political system. People in the organization are engaged in a continuous struggle for power, money, status. They're cogs but not robots. They mesh to the extent they have to in order to serve their individual ends, but not a great deal more. Also, organizations struggle with each other in the market place and the political arena. It follows that communication, oral and written, in and for the organization has a political aspect—political in the generic sense of a struggle for power and resources.

Real world writing, then, is functional in two different senses. It helps to keep the cogs meshing, and it serves the particular interests of the cogs and the bureaucracies as they struggle with each other for income, status, power. Impersonality is necessary for both functions. Political aims are more likely to be achieved if they are hidden. It is better to present one's case as necessary for smooth meshing of the cogs than as helpful in making my cog or my organization bigger than yours.

Therefore, the leading characteristic or requirement of successful writing in my real world is a relentless sort of clarity, impersonally expressed, and with a definite though partly hidden purpose. Its aim is neither truth nor beauty nor pleasure but action: to get readers to act in a way that serves the common ends of the organization and the particular ends of the writer and the other cogs on whom the writer most directly depends.

How does one achieve this functional and tendentious clarity? The key is what journalists call the story line. The story line is to expository writing what plot is to fiction. Good fiction, however, can have a minimum of plot or none at all. Think of Woody Allen's little film masterpiece, *Manhattan,* or Joseph Conrad's gem of a short novel, *The Shadow Line.* But good writing in the organization has invariably a clearly articulated line of argument that leads the reader on toward the conclusion the writer is trying to make him accept.

Obvious as this advice might seem, it is frequently honored in the breach. Recently, the top man in a big mid-West company gave a speech written for him by his staff. The final draft was beautifully written, as they say, by a master craftsman. It was full of interesting bits of information, embellished with historical allusions, each sentence and paragraph elegantly and sometimes wittily expressed. The speech was a dud. It made no argument and had no point. No one who listened to it or read it could tell what the conclusion was nor grasp the logic leading up to it. There was no story line.

To the real world writer, a story line rarely comes readymade. His assignment tells him the subject area and the political purpose of the writing. Discovering or inventing the story line is his responsibility. It's the biggest part of his job. Not long ago some colleagues and I in the Economics Department at Citibank got the assignment to write a little book about international banking and its principal contemporary manifestation, the Eurodollar market. The political aim was clear: to make a case for the social value of international banks and to argue against certain proposals for government regulation that would impair banks' efficiency. But what, exactly, did that mean? Were we to describe how international banking works, giving its historical background? Were we to outline the economic theory of banking and how it applies internally, thereby demonstrating that international banking is good for the people? Or were we to focus on the regulatory schemes that our opponents in the press, the Congress and the regulatory agencies were serving up and to demonstrate their inherent fallacies? Or was the argument to be some combination of all of these? Our various bosses were by no means of one mind on these questions. We had to decide for ourselves.

To make this decision we did what one must always do. For weeks that stretched into months we wallowed around in the subject, doing a lot of reading, getting our assistants to collect figures and help us with bibliography. We did a lot of talking and made a lot of outlines. We rough-drafted a chapter or two. But still we didn't know what the book was about. Finally, when we had reached a state of acute frustration, the decision made itself.

Obviously, to do all the things our bosses seemed to want, or all the things that might be done on the subject, would be to fill several big books that no reader we wanted to reach would read. We had to narrow and sharpen the focus drastically. So we decided to treat one issue, the one that promised the biggest political payoff: should the Eurodollar market be subject to a particular kind of regulation that had been proposed? Then, miraculously, everything fell into place. The relevance or irrelevance of all the research, the outlines and the rough-drafting became clear. We had found our focus, our story line, and now we could get down to the writing.

Finding the story line is often a sudden act of intuition. One must prepare the way for the welcome flash of insight by what is usally called research. I prefer to call it wallowing around in the subject. "Research" implies a clear-cut hypothesis one is trying to prove or disprove. The search for a story line is the search for a hypothesis. Only after one has formulated the story line with reasonable clarity is it possible to do research in the classic scientific sense, in order to see if the argument can withstand confrontation with hard facts. One can't do that until one has the argument in mind. The writer can spare himself a lot of anxiety if, in the early stages of the work, he admits frankly that he doesn't know what the piece is about, that he has no clear argument in mind and that the undirected and aimless character of his preliminary research is unavoidable and not a sign of feeblemindedness.

With the story line more or less in hand, the writer may sit down to draft an introduction. The result is often disappointing or worse. The line of argument that seemed so clear yesterday seems hazy this morning. This is the moment for another bit of psychological self-help. Lay that first, inadequate introduction aside and don't look at it again until you have forced your way through the first draft of the entire piece. Resist the temptation to rewrite the introduction. There is little chance that you will get the story line clear enough to foreshadow it in an introduction until you have worked through the whole argument at least once in the form of a complete draft.

Outlining at this early stage won't help much. An outline is the abstract form of a piece; more precisely, it is one possible form and probably not the final one. An outline is static while prose is dynamic. An outline is taken in at a glance, whereas reading a text takes time. The structure of an outline is simple, deductive, geometrical. The structure of a text—its story line—is like a river that follows the complex contours of the subject matter as it meanders through the countryside, though always remaining a single river, never losing its continuity from source to mouth. No simple, timeless shape, no purely deductive logical representation can capture such a movement through time. Indeed, one can't make an outline that really reflects the writing until the piece is finished and one no longer needs an outline except as a table of contents.

To my mind, outlining is most useful not at the beginning of a piece of writing but at intermediate stages, when an outline of what has already been drafted often helps to reveal a weakness or breakdown of the story line. Whenever I feel that a piece of writing is falling apart, that I am losing the thread, that I don't know what to say next or where this or that point comes in, I put it aside for a few days. Then I read it through as fast as possible and outline what is there. Frequently, the source of the trouble shows up clearly.

Another useful way of checking for a breakdown of the story line is to go back over the draft and take a hard look at the main transitions, the sentences and paragraphs that begin and end the various sections and chapters. Here is where a lot of trouble shows up. The transitions don't transish. They don't lead the reader from one point in a coherent story line to the next. They lead the reader off course, or they jump to a new subject without any apparent reason.

At this point the writer must stop and ask himself: "Just where am I in the basic argument I thought I was making? What exactly do the two points I'm trying to connect have to do with the conclusions I'm trying to lead the reader to?" Very often the honest answer is, "I don't exactly know." Then, even though his deadline is tomorrow and he is already late for dinner, the writer must lay down his pencil and find the answer to these questions before writing another word.

In this struggle to get the transitions right, a good editor is worth his or her weight in gold, at $800 an ounce. Editors I know often say, "The trouble is right here. It doesn't track." It's a good metaphor. Good real world writing stays on track all the time, from sentence to sentence, paragraph to paragraph, section to section. And the conclusion and introduction mirror each other. No gaps in the argument are allowed. Side trips to admire the scenery are discouraged lest the reader lose his way or tire himself out before he reaches his—your—conclusion. Like a sailboat well designed for cruising, with a long keel and not too much curve to the sides, a good piece of real world writing is almost self-steering. It doesn't demand of the reader that he be constantly watching the compass and adjusting the helm to keep from wandering off course.

Getting back on track is often just a matter of changing slightly the emphasis of a transitional sentence or paragraph, so that it refers back to the point just made and foreshadows the next step in the argument. It's astonishing how often the change of a word or two, or turning a sentence around, can clarify to the reader the point you have reached in the argument and carry him on to the next point. Such transitional words as "moreover," "furthermore," "however," "also," "then" and "now," or a minimal "but" or "and," at the beginning of a paragraph, can often bridge a gap into which readers may otherwise stumble. The real world writer has to sweat over transitions. They are where the men get separated from the boys, and the women from the girls.

Transitions, crucial as they are, should be unobtrusive. Often in a struggle to clarify a story line I find that some transitions have been overworked. In the course of conscientious rewriting, what is superfluous will become obvious. A phrase or sentence can now make the transition where before a paragraph or page seemed necessary. The logical structure of the piece now stands out by itself, and the scaffolding that helped the early drafting can be removed. In good, persuasive bureaucratic writing—unlike a scientific paper or a lawyer's brief—the bones don't show.

In such writing, spareness and austerity are also virtues. I do not mean exaggerated brevity, but understatement, a low emotional key. In the organization, persuasiveness is inversely proportional to the decibel level. The demagogue, the charismatic leader of a mob, the operatic soprano may get mileage from the power of the high-pitched voice to convey excitement, anger, grief. Renata Tebaldi's scream in the last act of *Tosca*, when she sees that her lover is not feigning death, is unforgettable. But written argument in the organization, or spoken, for that matter, had best be underplayed, lest the reader be moved to disbelief, resentment or an ironic smile. The real world writer who thinks he can bludgeon readers into submission by overstatement garnished with hyperbolic adjectives and adverbs reveals his ignorance or perhaps his own lack of conviction. A recent article on the Eurodollar market would have us believe that, "This vast sea of liquidity is ceaselessly swept by speculative storms and turbulence. Its hyperinflationary potential is so enormous that it quite literally threatens to destroy not only the dollar but every other paper currency as well." How could it be that bad?

Overargument is no better than overstatement and a good deal more tedious. A single line of reasoning that clinches the point, or one hard fact that is inconsistent with any conclusion but the writer's, will usually be more convincing than many. In a series of arguments, some will be better than others, and the weaker ones will lower the average. Add-on or make-weight arguments are particularly to be avoided. They may be inconsistent with the principal point, and the reader will be left with the impression that the writer is insincere or is trying to overpower by sheer quantity of argument. One good argument, then, is usually better than two. Which reminds me of the young lady who replies that she is not that kind of girl and besides the grass is wet.

One more how-to point. Nothing blurs the clarity of a story line more effectively than excessive use of figures, tables and diagrams. When I see a draft bristling with numbers, mine eyes glaze over, as they used to say on Madison Avenue. Arithmetical exercises and equations can be even worse. Anything that stops the rapid progression of the reader's thought, anything that makes him stop to work out or translate into his own language, is bad news. Bad news, that is for you, the writer. Either you'll lose the reader then and there, or if he's a conscientious fellow or anxious to prove to himself that he's as smart as you are, he will stop and work his way through the puzzle—and lose track of the story line. Then the phone rings and after hanging up, the reader, now subconsciously bored from the effort of mastering your clever equation, lays your piece aside never to pick it up again. Tables, diagrams, equations should be extracurricular, like footnotes, unnecessary to look at in order to follow the argument.

Good, clear writing of the kind I've been talking about may be dull. "Clarity is not the prize in writing," say Strunk and White, "nor is it the principal mark of good style.... But since writing is communication, clarity can only be a virtue."[2] And nowhere more so than in the organization. The ideal is to let unvarnished facts speak for themselves or appear to do so. Readers are presumed to have a business or professional interest in the subject. They need not be enticed by the writer's charm or swayed by his emotive power. Indeed, these qualities are inappropriate or embarrassing in the grey culture of the organization.

Would that it were otherwise, that one could say of good bureaucratic writing what C. E. Montague said of literary composition:

> ... clearness in the narrow sense—the thin lucidity of what passes at times for scientific statement—is not enough.... [The writer should seek] to raise mere logical precision to higher powers of veracity by mobilizing the subtler evocative values of words, their richness in secondary suggestion, their capacity to stimulate in the reader intuitive faculties more penetrative than formal reasoning. In his intercourse with readers [such a writer] will satisfy Newman's famous definition of a gentleman as one who never inflicts pain: he will always try to be good company, to make you at home and at ease and pleased with yourself.[3]

Indeed, the trouble with good real world writing as I have defined it is more than aesthetic. In the complexities of human affairs, the "indiscriminate use of clearness" is not necessarily the way to truth. But, again, writing in the organization is not a search for truth. Its purpose is to argue for a conclusion already reached by an administrative and political process whose aim is not truth but action.

Gentlemen in Newman's sense are out of fashion in the organization and ladies too, no doubt. G. K. Chesterton was closer to the mark when he said that a gentleman is never unintentionally rude. So perhaps the highest standard the real world writer can aim for is that clarity by which facts seem to speak for themselves. If he achieves it, it will be by dint of hard labor. For facts don't speak for themselves. They are dumb as dead Caesar's wounds awaiting a Marc Antony to give them tongues. But don't use that sort of simile when you write for the organization.

Notes

[1] *The Elements of Style* (New York, The Macmillan Co., 1959), p. 66.
[2] Strunk and White, p. 65.
[3] *A Writer's Notes on His Trade* (Garden City, New York: Doubleday, Doran & Co., 1930), p. 182.

10

Writing for the Human Services

MIRIAM MELTZER OLSON

Miriam Meltzer Olson holds an M.S.S.A. degree from Western Reserve University and a D.S.W. from the City University of New York. She practiced social work and, as a Fulbright scholar in England, did research in the field of mental health. She taught at Columbia and Fordham Universities, has been a consultant in the fields of health, child welfare, and education as well as mental health, and has written on health care and social services for women. She is currently Associate Professor of Social Administration at Temple University.

Much of the work of human service professionals (educators, physicians, rehabilitation counselors, social workers, nurses, probation officers, psychologists and the like) is done within organizations. The organizational context makes it necessary for them to communicate with other professionals and be accountable to the organization, in addition to communicating with and being accountable to their clients. To manage these necessities in day-to-day operations, human service professionals are called upon to do a good deal of writing. The writing requires of them, no more nor less than anyone else who writes, logic, clarity, specificity, and all the other qualities that we have come to associate with effective prose. Their writing is distinguished, though, by the part their reports play in determining specific courses of events in the lives of individuals. Human service professionals make and communicate judgments about their clients' personalities, social and economic circumstances, intelligence, motivations, disabilities, aspirations, vulnerabilities, relationships, and more. The judgments they present in their reports form the basis for deciding such matters as the suitability of a couple to adopt a child, the likelihood that a felon will engage in further criminal activity, the need of a single father for financial assistance, the possibility that a person might attempt suicide, the capacity of an aged person to care for herself, the neglectfulness of a child's parents, the ability of a stroke patient to recover lost speech, the stability of an individual to withstand the emotional trauma of an organ transplant. Their judgments also form the basis for deciding about the advantages of one type of service over another: special classes vs. "normal" classes for children with educational problems, family counseling and homemaker services vs. foster home placement for neglected children, for example.

It is clearly the case, then, that human service professionals have considerable power over their clients. Their power comes from several sources. One, of course, is their expertise. Another less commonly recognized source of power is in certain controls that professionals have over resources such as adoptable children, financial assistance, and therapies. The scarcer the resource, the greater the influence professionals may have in determining who gets what. For example, before there was universal coverage through Medicaid for the costs of hemodialysis and enough dialysis equipment and trained staff, patients were subject to intense psychological and social evaluation so that not only their medical condition, but also their emotional and social stability determined whether or not they received the treatment. Now, with dialysis available to all regardless of ability to pay, personal and family problems may raise questions, but patients are rarely refused treatment if it is medically indicated.

A third source of power comes from the fact that professionals whose services are provided through organizations serve two constituencies. They are responsible to the people who fund and determine the conditions for giving service, and to their clients as well. Often, the interests of the two are not the same, and the professionals act in the interest of the sponsoring organization. For instance, elderly people usually dread the prospect of having to go to a nursing home and see it as a place to die. Hospitals which are under public pressure to keep costs down discharge patients as soon as the medical or surgical need for hospitalization ends. Many elderly do not have relatives who can give them the care they need during the post-hospital recovery period, and they are referred to nursing homes. Since the need for hospitalization, even for non-fatal illnesses or injuries such as bone fractures, heightens elderly people's fear of permanent disability or death, they often understand a referral to a nursing home to mean that their condition is more serious than they have been told. It is not uncommon that patients who go to nursing homes make a poor recovery or even deteriorate. Thus, the interests of elderly patients would be better served if their hospital stay were lengthened to allow them recovery time, time for staff to help them sort out the facts of their condition from their fantasies, or to work out alternative plans for friends, church volunteers or others to help them at home. However, in order to serve the interests of the hospital, the professionals may use their influence to persuade patients that a nursing home is the best place for them.

People generally come into contact with human service professionals at a point of some distress or vulnerability in their lives. Professional codes of ethics recognize this and hold professionals to standards of conduct designed to prevent them from exploiting their clients' vulnerability. I would argue that the power disparity between professionals and clients increases clients' vulnerability, and that professionals have an additional ethical obligation to actively seek to minimize that disparity.

Human service professionals often don't appreciate how much power they have and that their clients are at a disadvantage as a result. They usually bring to their work a concern for the well-being of others, compassion and a desire to help. Since the helping activity they engage in depends in such large measure on establishing relationships of trust and confidence with their clients, it is in the interest of both the professionals and the people in need of human services that the professionals be aware of the power inequities and take responsibility to eliminate their negative consequences wherever possible.

The reports that human service professionals write reflect and often contribute to the problems created by the power disparity. The fact that written reports are sometimes the only form of communication used to evaluate clients' needs and make service recommendations compounds the problems. In my view, the teaching of writing can play a part in clarifying the ethical issues and mitigating existing problems. By helping students to develop skill in writing, both teachers of writing and teachers of the human service disciplines can make an important contribution to the understanding and competence with which students approach their responsibility for ethical professional conduct.

There are three major kinds of reports that human service professionals write. The first is evaluations. These are used primarily to establish a client's need for service and the type and amount to be provided. Some evaluations may be made on the basis of a single brief interview. Others may involve a test or a series of tests, or extended observation and interaction, or a combination of these. The second kind of report includes summaries and referrals. These are generally written when the services of a specific individual (such as a vocational counselor) or agency (such as a hospital) are terminated or when services beyond the scope of an individual discipline or agency are deemed necessary. Their purpose is to provide for continuity and coordination of care and aid.

Human service agencies need to attest to and justify the services they provide. They therefore need records which discuss not only the clients' circumstances but the staff's helping activities. Evaluations, referrals and summaries, which provide both types of information, may be used as instruments of accountability. However, since such reports often focus only on the clients, human service professionals may also be called upon to write activity reports. The purpose of this third type of record is to provide documentation of services provided and to indicate the effects and effectiveness of the services.

Ethical problems arise in the writing of all types of reports. One problem derives from the very nature of judgment making. The conclusions professionals draw about what is going on in their clients' lives, what should be done about it, and what results can be expected from the actions they take are affected by the professionals' notions about human events and causal relations in human affairs. Explanatory theories about human affairs are complex, incomplete, imprecise, diverse and even contradictory. Whatever the total effects are of living in a society where, for example, an adolescent's stealing may be understood as a product of an impaired superego, or immorality, or social and economic circumstances that block legitimate opportunities for success, or behavior learned through association with others, it is the case that professionals who deal with youngsters who steal have the responsibility for taking action despite the lack of consensus about stealing and how it should be treated. Acting in the face of uncertainty and ambiguity is a condition of professional practice. Even where there is a high degree of consensus, such as in certain branches of medicine, limits on what is known about a condition or knowable about the course a condition will take create the necessity to act without certainty.

At the same time, all professional practices are based on some systematized body of knowledge. The problem is that all professionals need to understand clearly the theoretical foundations on which their judgments are based and the assumptions on which they operate. The theoretical lenses through which human service professionals view service situations determine not only what they see, but what they choose to look at. I came across a situation that shows the influence of different theoretical perspectives on problem evaluation and prediction: A school's consulting psychiatrist referred an eight year old boy to a child guidance clinic for therapy because the child was not performing well in school and, in the psychiatrist's view, had emotional problems. The referral statement included the information that the child came from a working class family. The social worker at the child guidance clinic who saw the parents for an initial interview described them in her report as middle class. The questions which arise are why information about the family's social class was included by both professionals and why their classifications differed. When asked about the theoretical framework which guided his thinking, the psychiatrist said that classical psychoanalytic theory was the major source of his understanding. He was less well-informed about theory pertaining to social class, but did not think that class played a part in the etiology of the child's emotional disturbance. The working class designation was made because the father was employed as a factory worker. The psychiatrist admitted that he hadn't given a great deal of thought to the issue of social class and probably included his reference to it because he assumed that blue collar workers are not apt to be psychologically oriented or introspective. Thus the inclusion of this information reflected his expectation that the parents might not be much of a source for uncovering information about the child's problem nor be motivated to seek counseling for themselves.

The social worker, on the other hand, was guided by what she described as a social systems approach, emphasizing patterns of interaction in a social field. She understood social class as expected behavioral and attitudinal patterns related to social and economic factors. She identified the family as middle class on the basis of several such factors. For one thing, the family was black, and she believed that any consideration of occupational status had to take into account the limitations on opportunity resulting from racism.

She took the father's position as a plant foreman, given the particular factory in which he worked and the community in which the factory was located, as clear proof of a considerable achievement, and one which within the black community would have afforded him a higher status than his counterparts in the white community. She attached similar meaning to the fact that the mother worked as a secretary to a bank officer. In addition, she identified as influential in her thinking the fact that the children attended a parochial school. Maintaining religious affiliation and the shared norms of particular ethnic groups were common motivations for the white parents in the community to send their children to parochial school. Since neither of these were motivations here, the investment in the children's education suggested to her that the family had aspirations and expectations of achievement generally associated with middle class status. She believed that these aspirations and expectations would be imbued with special meaning for a black family, and that the child's school problems were likely to have a serious impact on him and the parents as well. Her expectation was that the parents would have a strong desire to deal with the problems.

In both instances, the professionals' assumptions about the implications of the family's social class remained to be tested against additional facts to be gathered about this particular family. Clarity about their frames of reference and the assumptions they made were essential, then, for responsible pursuit of fact. The lack of such clarity on the part of professionals increases the vulnerability of clients to being misunderstood. The judgment a professional makes can produce, among other things, self-fulfilling prophesies. If parents are perceived as willing partners in an effort to resolve a child's problem, they may be treated with the kind of regard that encourages their participation, whereas parents who are perceived as unlikely partners may not be and therefore receive poorer service.

A second ethical problem in the human services has to do with the place of values in professional practice. Just as all professional practices operate out of a knowledge base—a set of ideas about what is—so too are they guided by ideas about what is preferred in the conduct of human affairs. Because the relationship between knowledge and values is highly complex, because knowledge can alter values and values can influence the pursuit and selection of explanatory theories, an important aim for human service professionals is to be able to distinguish between knowledge and values and clearly identify the values on which they operate. This task is often obscured by the demand that professionals' judgments be objective and value-free. While it's a very obvious example, a case of a pregnant fourteen year old illustrates the issue of value bias. The youngster lived with her three sisters and thirty-year-old mother. The father had deserted the family, and their financial support came through public assistance. The obstetrician at the clinic the teenager attended recommended that she give the baby up for adoption and also have a tubal ligation to prevent further pregnancies. The school nurse with whom she discussed the situation when she became ill at school felt that she should accept her 17-year-old boyfriend's offer to marry her and keep the baby. The teacher in whom she confided encouraged her to consider having an abortion and not jeopardize her scholastic promise. All of the professionals offered recommendations that could be justified on "objective" grounds. However, the influence of different value orientations is apparent. Value preferences which operate more subtly, such as the preference nurses may have for patients who comply with hospital routines over those who raise questions, are no less significant in the effect they have on service to clients. It's necessary, then, that human services professionals consistently practice making their value positions explicit for themselves and others.

A third problem that affects writing has to do with the use of professional jargon. The special languages which professionals develop serve numerous purposes. They can be a form of shorthand that simplifies communication, particularly of technical information. At the same time, as with all special languages adopted by particular groups of people, they can serve to promote group identification and establish boundaries between the members of the group and outsiders. The mastery of an idiosyncratic vocabulary can also endow its users with a special status. Boundaries and status are frequently concerns of professionals such as educators, social workers and psychologists because their areas of expertise are subjects of intimate concern to the general public. Widespread claims to knowledge, wisdom and common sense about human affairs can undermine the professionals' authority. Jargon can be used then, to assert the legitimacy of the professionals' claim to expertise.

For clients, a problem with the professionals' use of jargon is that it can put them at a disadvantage by making knowledge inaccessible to them. The limiting effects which the use of jargon by physicians have on patients' ability to understand their own conditions and to hold physicians accountable to them have become familiar issues in public discussions of health care. The use of professionals' idiosyncratic vocabulary can also impede communication among members of different professional disciplines. Witness the following from a report of a pediatrician to a team of school consultants attempting to develop an educational plan for a child with learning difficulties.

> Bobby was a full-term 3 kg. product of an unremarkable gestation to a G3P2 27 y.o. WF. There were no perinatal difficulties and he was discharged at 4 days of age. He was fed similac without difficulty. Immu-

izations are up to date. There is a question of hay fever, but no known drug allergies. He was hospitalized X2 for bilateral inguinal herniorrhaphies. Growth and Development: Bobby sat at 4-5 months, stood @ 1 yr, walked @ 1 yr, talked @ 1 yr (sentences @ 2 yrs) toilet trained @ 4 yrs (with H/O soiling difficulties at age 7) rode tricycle @ 2-3 yrs.

The pressure in recent years for increased accountability of professionals to the people they serve plays a part in the final two ethical problems I want to talk about. They are the "labeling" of clients and clients' access to their own records.

Making a professional evaluation involves organizing data so that the specifics of a situation can be categorized in some useful way. The types of categories may be mandated by law. For instance, publicly funded and accredited mental health centers are required to assign psychiatric diagnoses to all persons using their help. The mandated use of a particular manual of diagnostic classification[1] is designed to minimize the differences in assessment discussed earlier, differences stemming from different theoretical orientations. However, minimizing clients' vulnerability to differing assessments does not eliminate the vulnerability that results from the assignment of a psychiatric diagnosis. Nor does it address the anomaly of assigning psychiatric diagnoses to all clients when one of the objectives of the Federal law which established community mental health centers[2] was to provide services to people experiencing personal or family difficulties in order to prevent the development of mental illness.

Similarly, the Federal law designed to assure equal educational opportunities for all handicapped children[3] requires that those with special learning needs be identified as learning disabled, educable mentally retarded, trainable mentally retarded, socially or emotionally disturbed and the like, in order to receive necessary services. The use of diagnostic labels, whether mandated by law or not, can have serious consequences. Psychiatric diagnoses, for example, can cost people jobs, insurance, driver's licenses and more. Diagnoses and other labels assigned to children, such as "aggressive" or "acting out" or "defiant of authority," have been shown to negatively prejudice their school careers and to contribute to their holding negative views of themselves.

The task of protecting clients from stigma is complicated, and the pejorative use that has been made of "clinical" nomenclature is a source of concern among many professionals as well as consumer groups. Their efforts to decrease vulnerability to damaging reports have resulted, for one thing, in groups such as parents of school children gaining the right to read their children's records. However, support for people's right to read their records is not unequivocal. Many university professors, for example, have voiced strong objection to permitting students to see their letters of reference. They argue that letters to which students have access will lack candor and therefore be of little use for admission or employment purpose. At present, applications to colleges and universities may ask students to waive their right to read their reference letters.

Human services professionals in other arenas perceive harm that could result from certain clients' reading their psychiatric or medical diagnoses or prognoses as well as dilemmas posed by the fact that information about a client may have been given in confidence by relatives or others. Even professionals who accept the principle of client access to records are of the opinion that it imposes undesirable constraints on them. A speech therapist, for example, who observed a father calling his child "dummy" and making disparaging remarks about his child's stammer was reluctant to record her concern that the father was having a negative influence on the child's progress. At the same time she recognized that failure to note the father's behavior could skew an evaluation of the child's response to the therapy provided.

It is clear that the ethical problems involved in labeling and access to records, like the other problems mentioned, are not simply problems in writing, and need to be tackled at a variety of political, professional and educational levels. Nevertheless, ways of handling such problems are intimately connected with writing skills; professionals who have skill and confidence in their ability to communicate in writing will be better able to present useful information to others that serves the purpose it's designed to serve and that minimizes the unintended and negative consequences reports can have. Both teachers of the professional disciplines and teachers of writing need to play a part in helping students develop the knowledge, skill and confidence to deal with the problems which writing for the human services poses.

To begin with, as my comments on theoretical orientation suggest, students need to learn to make informed assessments within the framework of an orienting body of knowledge. The responsibility for providing them with a theoretical framework belongs to the teachers of the professional disciplines. But students also need to learn about the problems in the process of arriving at and communicating their assessments, and both teachers of the professional disciplines and teachers of writing can help them understand and deal with those problems. For example, students need to be alerted to the circularity which is inherent in any effort to describe and anaylze human events. As people search for data to arrive at a coherent view of a situation, they are predisposed to observe, select, and report some data and not others. At the same time students need to learn, whether they are writing a composition, a research paper or a case report for professional purposes, that the problem of overlooking some information cannot be solved simply by expanding the amount of information included. The tasks of making an assessment and the tasks of preparing a research paper—collecting, ordering and giving meaning to facts, establishing relationships among them, assigning relative weights to their importance, determining causal connections and such—make selectivity unavoidable. Including more data makes reports unserviceable and uneconomical and weakens the conclusions they present.

Writing activities which draw students' attention to the handling of factual material can help them to understand the problems their biases create in the assessment process and help them to overcome them. For instance, it is useful to have them consider the different order of facts they use. There are facts which are verifiable, e.g., Mr. Jones drinks a quart of whisky a day, and those which depend on consensual agreement, e.g., Mr. Jones is an alcoholic. Clarity about this distinction can help students consider the audience for whom they are writing, and determine whether their reports will be read by people with shared understanding, or whether the use of a term like "alcoholic" needs to be supported by facts which explain it. Similarly, distinction needs to be drawn about the sources of the facts students present in their reports. There would be considerable difference between a referral for marriage counseling that states that Mr. Jones is an alcoholic and one that states that Mrs. Jones says her husband is an alcoholic.

The relationship of fact and inference is another important consideration for students. The assertion that Mrs. Smith is a poor housekeeper made by a caseworker investigating alleged child neglect and used to support the conclusion that the mother is neglectful, is questionable and potentially harmful if the facts from which the inference was drawn are not included. If the facts are that there were dirty dishes in the sink, roaches in the kitchen, piles of dirty clothes and drafts in the children's bedroom from broken windows, the inference could be challenged. Perhaps there was no hot water in the apartment, and the conditions the case worker observed reflected the landlord's failure to maintain the building properly.

In addition to writing activities, the reading of case reports can help students with the problem of bias. The use of a report such as the one which follows should help students from different disciplines or orientations see how the writer arrived at his conclusions, whether they would come to the same conclusions based on the facts presented, whether the facts were sufficient to support the inferences drawn and whether causal relationships were adequately established.

Name: Thomas Woods

Charge: Aggravated assault with intent to kill.

Description of Incident: Woods took part in a fight between two youth groups. The fight broke out in the parking lot of Dewey High School following a basketball game. Woods inflected injuries on one youth. The youth sustained a fractured skill and a ruptured kidney.

Record: No prior arrests

Recommendation: Probation

Summary: Thomas Woods is a 17-year-old white male in the 12th grade of Dewey High School. He lives with his mother and 14-year-old brother. His father died of emphysema six months ago.

The charge against Woods is his first offense. There is no pattern of delinquent behavior. His involvement in the fighting incident was probably due to the stress the boy has been under. He had to adjust to the death of his father. He also had to adjust to a new school and making new friends. His family moved back to Gotham when the father died. They lived in Denver for three years prior for the father's health.

Woods' school record shows satisfactory academic performance and no problems of truancy or insubordination. He began to associate with the other boys involved in the fight about three weeks before the incident.

Woods shows remorse over the injuries he caused. He understands the seriousness of his action and does not project blame on anyone else. The boy comes from a religious family and attends church.

Mrs. Brown is also under stress due to her husband's death and is working to support the family. She appears to be a very concerned mother and is upset over Tom's behavior. She describes her son as a very bright boy who has always been well-liked by family, friends and teachers. She says he is fun-loving and adventurous but he never caused her any trouble. He also showed responsibility during his father's illness. He helped with chores and worked at part-time jobs. He doesn't have any unusual problems getting along with his mother for a boy his age.

Woods also has a close-knit extended family in Gotham. The family goes back for four generations. They are a civic-minded family and there is no history of any involvement with the law. The paternal grandmother and a maternal aunt and uncle have offered to supervise Tom and his brother while the mother is at work.

Overall Impression: Thomas Woods appears to be a boy from a family with high standards of conduct who incorporated those standards for himself. Due to the emotional shock of his father's death and inadequate direction he got involved with the wrong crowd. With the support of his family and the supervision of a probation officer he should get the direction he needs and a positive male image to identify with.

Discussion of this report could help students consider what the probation officer's underlying assumptions were and whether, in fact, a coherent framework for analysis could be discerned. They should find that despite the authoritativeness of the report, there's a vagueness. Stress, emotional shock and lack of direction are identified as the cause of the delinquent act. Church attendance, remorse, the lack of a criminal record or school difficulties and the family's high standards of conduct are identified as countervailing forces. The provision of supervision and a positive male image are identified as the necessary conditions to shift the balance of influences from the stress-induced behavior to socially accepted behavior. Yet neither the particular notions about "emotional shock" nor the parole's officers view of the relationship between emotional shock and delinquent behavior are spelled out. In addition, some students might find the lack of information about the client's early development a problem in making a prediction. Others might want to know more about the school and the neighborhood in which the boy lived. There might be disagreement about the parole officer's assumption about the need for male identification, and so on.

Examination of such a report could help students with the issue of value bias as well as theoretical bias. Thus, with this report, students' attention could be drawn to the question of whether the perception that the youth came from a "good family" influenced the selection of data, the weight given the family factors, the expectation that the family could exert positive influence over his behavior, and the recommendation for probation itself.

In teaching students about the problems of bias through case reports, I've found it helpful, after discussing the theoretical and value issues, to have the students identify what the report tells them about the client and what it tells them about the person who wrote it. I find that this generally results in the students' weighing their reports more carefully and also reading the reports of others with greater discernment.

Precision in language and sensitivity to the resonances of words are other qualities of effective writing students can be taught. A report written by a school psychologist illustrates the effect of lack of skill in these areas. The psychologist evaluated a ten-year-old boy who had been in special classes since first grade because of delays in learning, extreme distractability and "bizarre" behavior—blinking, finger snapping and choking himself. At the point he was referred for reevaluation he was reading at the second grade level although he had an unusually large vocabulary compared to other children his age in his school. He had an avid interest in creatures from outer space and prehistoric animals, and had considerable knowledge about them. His teachers felt they did not understand his learning problems or needs well enough to provide an individualized educational program for him. The psychologist's report included the following:

> Willy is a cute and precocious 10-year-old boy with striking blue eyes and a shock of unruly blond hair. He is the third of four children and presently lives with his mother and two siblings. Although Willy appears to be a bright child, he has never worked up to an academic level commensurate with his intelligence. As a result he has known a motley collection of educational placements, including a regular kindergarten and resource rooms, as well as classrooms for the learning disabled and socially and emotionally disturbed.

The use of "precocious" in this excerpt from the school psychologist's report highlights the issue of word selection. "Precocious" is defined as "forward in development, especially mental development; prematurely developed, as the mind, faculties, etc."[4] Its use by a school psychologist in an evaluation of a child with unusual learning patterns is extremely important. If the child is forward in his mental development, he might be in need of stimulation and enrichment provided through programs for the gifted. However, there were no findings included in the report to substantiate the claim of precocity nor to account for poor performance relative to a prematurely developed mind. The report lacked specific facts about Willy's mental development and about the instruments used to measure his intellectual capacity. These lacks, compensated for only by the rather imprecise statement that Willy appears to be "bright," make the assertion that he is precocious highly questionable. Given the lack of precision and specificity in this report and the rest of the language used to describe Willy ("cute," "striking blue eyes," a "shock of unruly blond hair"), the word "precocious" would appear not to have been used denotatively, but to serve the purpose of communicating the psychologist's positive response to the boy.

Recognition of the connotative meanings carried by words is important for students. Numerous words used by human service professionals carry negative connotations. "Unmotivated" and "resistant" have specific technical meanings, but they are frequently used in a manner analogous to the school psychologist's use of "precocious." That is, they're presented within a technical context, but without careful regard for their technical meaning. A report that states that Mrs. Green is unmotivated to attend parent-teacher conferences may convey the impression that Mrs. Green is deficient as a parent. Similarly, a patient who does not follow the advice of a rehabilitation counselor and is reported to be resistant to treatment may be viewed as a "bad" patient and no longer provided with services.

The liberation movements of recent years have contributed to a heightened awareness of language. They can provide useful lessons with particular relevance for human service professionals to illustrate the importance of the resonances of words. Examination of the issues involved in the current and past uses of the words "Negro" and "black," "girl," "lady" and "woman," "disabled" and "handicapped," as well as terms such as "illegitimate child" and "unwed mother," can provide students with insight into the power words have not only to convey meaning but to create impressions and evoke feelings.

The last quality of writing that I will talk about here is style. I have expressed concern about the various ways that the reports written by human service professionals can affect the power disparity between them and their clients. I have mentioned some of the responsibilities I believe professionals have for writing reports that minimize clients' vulnerability to their power. At several points I spoke of the importance of recognizing the problems of bias and dealing with them by making the biases apparent. Accurate communication of facts, precision and specificity are some of the means identified for exposing a professional's biases to others. But even these measures do not eliminate the communication of opinions and impressions. Nor do I think that professionals can or should eliminate them. My concern is with the manner in which impressions and opinions are recorded. The dominant trend in the writing of professional reports is to avoid personal references. Some social workers, for example, handle this by referring to their own activities or observations in the third person. They might say that "the worker gave Mr. White an application for Medicaid" or that "it was the worker's impression that Mr. White felt ashamed that he needed assistance." Other professional reports eliminate references to the writer altogether. They might say that "Mr. White was given a Medicaid application" or that "Mr. White evidenced shame at the need for assistance." This impersonal style is aimed at establishing the professional credibility of the writer by conveying objectivity. Yet my point is that regardless of how scrupulously professionals attempt to achieve objectivity, their efforts are necessarily limited. Detachment from the writing and heavy reliance on professional jargon serve to create uniformity among reports that further suggests greater authority and certainty than is possible for their writers. Of course, for all the efforts at uniformity and objectivity, biases are revealed and individual styles are apparent. I believe students need to be helped to accept and unmask the limits of their own objectivity, and to claim their own contribution to their reports.

Having learned to consciously reveal themselves through the deliberate incorporation of the qualities of effective report writing discussed here, students should be better prepared not only to meet the ethical obligations their reports require, but also to deal with the fundamental issues of theory, values and organizational influences which create the power disparities between human service professionals and their clients and the ethical problems that result.

Notes

[1] *Diagnostic and Statistical Manual of Mental Disorders,* third edition (Washington, D. C.: American Psychiatric Association, 1980).

[2] Public Law 88-164, Mental Retardation Facilities and Community Mental Health Centers Construction Act of 1963, 88th Congress, October 1, 1963.

[3] Public Law 94-142, Education for All Handicapped Children Act of 1975, 94th Congress, November 29, 1975.

[4] *The Random House Dictionary of the English Language* (New York: Random House, 1968).

11

Teaching Writers at a Government Agency

JOHN R. ADAMS

John R. Adams is a manager in the planning and budgeting office at the U. S. Environmental Protection Agency. Before joining the Agency, he worked as a technical editor with two consulting firms. His undergraduate degree is in symbolic logic, and his Ph.D. from the University of Pennsylvania is in linguistics. He prepared this article in his private capacity. No official support or endorsement by the Environmental Protection Agency or any other agency of the Federal government is intended or should be inferred.

A memo crossed my desk recently: "One of the major costs associated with our telephone system is the number of voice instruments used in the Agency."

"Voice instruments?" Later I discovered that whoever wrote that spellbinding phrase was trying to refer to the telephones we all know and love, as opposed to data telephones. But kazoos are voice instruments, too.

On another occasion, I worked with a group developing what was called the Bubble Policy. The Bubble was a clever metaphor for a complicated way to treat sources of air pollution (by placing an imaginary bubble over the facility). Our *Federal Register* notice called the policy an "Alternative Approach to Pollutant Emission Limitations."

Yes, writers in the government can write wretchedly, as we all have seen. I can think of several authors who have made reasonable livings poking fun at examples of opaque prose and hideous words in governmental writing. I would poke fun too, except I believe that most groups have their share of ugly words; my academic discipline, linguistics, has little room to complain when it uses technical terms like *morphophoneme* or *gerundival*.

Of course, we can easily train government employees to shift styles a bit when they write for the public. Training like that is usually only cosmetic, however, requiring little more than spelling out acronyms and explaining other shorthand expressions that are more prevalent in the government than in ordinary writing. These cosmetic quick fixes at the level of substituting definitions or eliminating a few well-publicized ugly words are not very effective, however. Strict rules about those superficial problems can even lead writers astray. Once, for example, I saw a letter addressed to the newly appointed head of a government agency. It ran, in part, "Congratulations on being appointed to the Federal Aviation Administration (FAA)." I think the new Commissioner could have worked out the acronym for his own agency.

Rather, I have found that the problems with government writing should be attacked much more systematically than merely pointing out a few ugly terms like "voice instrument," or "alternative approach," or other shorthand references that spring up within all small groups of specialists. I have tried to help writers learn to use more fundamental, systematic devices to improve their organization and syntax in writing. I developed these devices mainly from my experience with people who prepared briefings for management. Two others and I then collected the devices, together with methods to improve other mechanics of writing, into a publication for the Environmental Protection Agency, "Be a Better Writer: A Manual for EPA Employees." Here are the highlights of what we recommend:

Organizing Systematically

Most people, surprisingly, don't organize their writing well. I don't mean to say that my coworkers have deficient academic credentials—far from it—but rather that they haven't been taught how to organize. I can speak from experience because one of my jobs for a time was to sit down with young staffers and help them perfect their organization for briefings and written papers.

Before I analyzed the problems in organizing, I would have thought that the best approach would be to use common sense—put things in a reasonable order and get on with your business. Not so. Most academically trained writers fail to get their points across fast enough. The organizational style that tells 'em quick, putting conclusions at the front and substantiating them later, is a strikingly effective contrast to the static or taxonomic structure that places facts in categories and then stops. That slow style may carefully adduce facts, but it plays peek-a-boo until the end, when all of the conclusions (or issues, or recommendations) lie flaccid on the page, frequently without the support they need.

That style is hard to wade through, places much too much paper ahead of what a manager is looking for (economy of crucial information is important to managers, even if economy of total information isn't a governmental strongpoint), and saps the logical support for the conclusions.

I know the human nature behind writing that way. It's easy to tell what you did on a study: Week One you traveled, Week Two you looked at numbers, Week Three you talked to people. Writing a report that follows chronology is easy—it simply reports what *you* did. Except it's what your *boss* should do that's more important. Finally, usually at 2:00 a.m. the night before the piece is due, you sit down to write conclusions and find that Fact 7 on Page 9 was the crucial one and it ought to be closer to your conclusion. But it's somewhere, isn't it, so why reorganize the piece, and it's time to go to bed anyway.

The way to counteract that human nature is to turn most early organizations upside down, or at least sideways. For example, once I was doing a study of government reponse to spills of hazardous substances—stuff like bulk chlorine or raw materials for plastics or even waste material. We had several ways to go about organizing the study and the report. For example, it turned out that there were three kinds of substances spilled: oil products, substances covered "normally" under the water act (for shorthand, we used the section of law that applied to them—Section 311), and more difficult spills covered elsewhere ("Section 504" for short).

On the other hand, we could organize the report around the actors: state employees, industry, or the Feds, which we subdivided into the Environmental Protection Agency and other Federal agencies. Different members of our team examined these areas.

In either case, how we organized the study, or even the four-volume report summarizing it, wasn't necessarily the way we should have organized the Executive Summary for the study. In that paper, we paid particular attention to our recommendations, which cut diagonally through the material to include points on information systems, on funding, and on how EPA could improve.

That method of organizing had the additional benefit of avoiding a "looping," inelegant method that guarantees covering your topic at the risk of repeating yourself. To take either of the two ways we had prepared the study—describing the types of spills or the actors—would have left us repeating material on, say, oil every time we moved to a different actor: what the states do about oil, then later what industry does about it, then .... Our solution clustered the information in an entirely different way—namely, describing what our administrator needed to do. It didn't simply repeat the categories of substance we studied or recite the actors involved.

People frequently resist the style of organization that emphasizes recommendations. They do so, I think, because it requires them to do something twice, first understanding the facts and then reorganizing around the important facts. After all, getting something organized the first time *is* a feat; to do it again in a different shape can be more work than many writers are prepared to invest. Moreover, the distinction among themes for organizing is sometimes subtle and without a direct appeal to authority; there are no clearcut rules.

One way to cope with the human nature of not wanting to change, however, is to have a writer find someone to help with the organizing before any outline is down on paper. The timing is important, though. Speculating on how a paper would sound it if were organized in such and such a way is easier when the points are still fluid. Once the moving finger has writ, it moves on.

Even after a paper is in outline form, there are still ways for improving technique. One is to force the major points to the front even if they're not recommendations. Telling junior staffers that their recommendations should start off their papers—naked!—frequently makes them nervous. In hierarchical workplaces, junior members frequently feel that they shouldn't be telling the boss what to do. They don't have recommendations, they lay out "just the facts, ma'am," so that people up the ladder can make the right choice. I've found that their managers really want to know what they should do. Organizing more tightly can highlight the most important points inside the piece as "major issues" rather than "recommendations." It's an antidote to burying major points deep inside a subtopic.

Selecting a different organizing principle (recommendations or major issues over simple categories of facts, for example) adds a new overall structure to the report. Once that structure is fixed, there is still room for systematic approaches within the main framework.

Take lists. Everywhere I've worked, I've found that most writers use bullets galore. (Bullets are little filled-in circles like this ● used to set off separate items in a list.)

- Like
- This.

Writing with bullets is easy if you don't have much to say: just slap down several unrelated facts and you've filled a page. A more systematic approach, however, requires that the writer consider how the bulleted items are related and why they are in that order. People usually have a flow in mind when they write something. But what finally hits the page may no longer appear connected, partly because this method of writing encourages putting points down in the first order that comes to mind. The easiest way to spot this slapdash style is to notice the setup paragraph preceding the bullets. If it reads like this,

> The following features have been identified:

or, worse,

> The features are:

it suggests that whoever wrote the setup put down a disorganized collection of facts. If, on the other hand, there's an organizing principle encompassing the list, you've found a good organizer:

> The following discussion will move from those two groups closer to the problem through the layers of management to the top decision makers ....

A similar matter has to do not so much with the theme as with the order of the list. The first item, for example, always enjoys a special advantage for the very reason that it's first. Using the "mechanical" trick of asking the maker of the list the reason for first one item, then another, usually elicits what was the implicit organizing principle. Any number of principles can work, from simple time sequence, to some standard order, to one that puts the most important one first. (Some people call the last way "prioritizing"— good idea, ugly word.) The way I approach organizing is to apply "mechanical" techniques that begin independently of content but lead, with work, to a more useful presentation. That approach won't help everyone; for example, behind it is an assumed minimum competence in written English. But the people I work with in the government have that competence. They work with words for a living; the fecundity of their word formations is just one evidence of that.

Editing Syntax Systematically

We tried to present in "Be a Better Writer" a fresh approach to systematic problems with writing. That approach brought in many of the principles of transformational grammar, but not the type that normally appears in courses titled "Modern Grammar." Modern syntactic theory describes language in two steps: a part that discusses sentence forms (usually called "phrase structure") and a part that shows systematic relations between the forms (the "transformational" component). People who are good at sentence diagramming can usually master the basic ideas behind phrase structure in a hurry. Although the principles behind the two approaches are different, they appear remarkably similar in practice. Transformations, on the other hand, represent systematic connections between pairs of sentences. We usually use phrase structure in talking about transformations, but it's not mandatory. In fact, most courses dwell too long on phrase structure at the expense of transformations. I think that might be the case because textbooks frequently define transformations using "math talk." Who cares that "transformation" is borrowed from algebra? Linguistic transformations are patterns that come naturally to anybody who talks.

The classic example of a transformation is the passive. We speak of an operation (the "passive transformation") that rearranges the words in

John wrote this sterling piece of poetry.

while leaving the meaning unchanged:

This sterling piece of poetry was written by John.

Note that the terminology is dynamic. We speak of turning one sentence into another in a regular way. We can even apply a mathematical notation to show the relationship and help describe the inevitable exceptions. Understanding the notation, however, is not a prerequisite for understanding the principles behind transformations.

Transformations are notoriously hard to describe systematically. Even the passive, perhaps the simplest transformation to grasp and certainly the most frequently cited, has numerous counterinstances. Following the pattern would yield

Yesterday at noon was arrived by Mary
—Yecch!—from

Mary arrived yesterday at noon.

Counterexamples (in this case, intransitive verbs and adverbial nouns) pile up. Moreover, there's a subtle change in meaning or emphasis between an active and its passive counterpart.

Most of the theoretical discussions in linguistics have to do with finding out why all those counterexamples spring up. But the goals of the theoretician are different from what concerns us here. People know how to spot a counterexample because it "sounds funny"; we needn't worry about how they do it.

In the 1960s, linguists also proposed transformations that didn't link sentences, so that a nominalization (also now called a "nominal") would result from a noun-forming transformation:

George prepared the manuscript

turns into

George's preparation of the manuscript

Also related are "passive-like" versions which have subject and object reversed and the familiar *by* phrase:

The preparation of the manuscript by George . . .

The manuscript preparation by George . . .

The basic pattern is to create a noun phrase (containing *preparation* in the example) from a full sentence. Further operations can intervene to shuffle other portions of the original sentence.

Transformations can be thought of as working in both directions. We can speak of undoing a nominalization if we pass from

The regulation promulgation by the Agency

to any of the following, using the same patterns as in the example with George and the manuscript:

The promulgation of the regulation by the Agency . . .

The Agency's promulgation of the regulation . . .

The Agency promulgated the regulation.

An editor would be just as surprised as Moliere's character (when he learned he'd been speaking prose all that time) to discover that much of editing is simply applying or undoing transformations and using subjective criteria about what sounds better. Our approach was to get our writers to use a systematic method, which we dressed up as the Red Flag Approach to Editing (that is, always try to edit certain constructions). We used the Red Flag Approach on our old friend the passive, which everyone dislikes, and on my own pet peeve, overworked nominalizations.

Systematically Examining Passives

Everyone rails against the passive voice as a prime contributor to murky writing. Government writing exudes sentences like these:

It is recommended that . . .
Implementation is expected to begin . . .
Credit was given to the company for . . .

We've all heard the objections, and I subscribe to most of them: passive is less forceful than active; it tends to suppress the actor, making it difficult to divine Who Did What; it adds extra words; overusing it leads to a monotonous style without focus.

Our problem when writing our manual was how far to go as we inveighed against the passive. One friend wanted to prohibit it totally, to write a rule saying Use No Passive Voice. (Incidentally, we had several people stop using past tense, trying to avoid the passive.) A rule is certainly clean; perhaps it is a reasonable goal. But I know government writers. They look for loopholes. Are these examples any better than the passives I just mentioned?

The following recommendation obtains . . .
The expected commencement of implementation will happen . . .
Company credit for . . . occurred.

Maybe I've been co-opted by too many years in the government, but I merely twitch when I read the plain passive; the ague sets in when I read the second set of examples. Yet the second set would follow a No Passive rule. We invoked the Red Flag to help our readers decide when to untangle a passive and when to leave well enough alone.

To prepare our readers for the Red Flag Approach, we went on for some time trying to make it clear how to identify a passive phrase. That meant first defining a past participle like *proposed* (after overcoming the mindblock over that grammar term) and then identifying two other marks of a passive that are not always present. We called those two marks the "form of *be*" and the "*by* phrase" carrying the agent. We used these examples:

Regulations on this topic *will be* propos*ed by* EPA [all three marks present]

Regulations on this topic *will be* propos*ed* in six months [missing the *by* phrase]

Regulations propos*ed* before 1979 will help the Agency avoid litigation [only participle present]

So far, we had hardly done more than repeat sixth grade grammar. Our next step was to introduce a systematic approach—the Red Flag. We asked our writers to pause (at the imaginary flag) when reading a passive construction, then to test it by changing it into an active. Behind this approach was our belief that, given a choice between a passive construction and its active counterpart, our readers would make the right one.

From a theoretical point of view, what we were suggesting is difficult to to describe. For example, not every word ending in *-ed* (ignoring past tense forms) should be called a past participle (thus to raise the Red Flag and cause an editor to consider its active counterpart). In the phrase *a complicated idea* it seems silly to ask, "Who complicated the idea?" yet I would ask, "Who proposed?" in *a proposed regulation.* These examples suggest that "adjective" (no Red Flag) and "participle" (test the active) aren't so easy to define in all cases. But in practice, our audience would know which phrases to test. They don't need a large bank of exceptions. We also expected them to leave some passives alone because they "sound better." In fact, we went on for some time suggesting occasions when the passive is a better choice (for placement of transitions, for general sentences when an agent like "someone" is irrelevant, as in *The tissue sample was dissected and soaked for 24 hours,* and for general aesthetics).

Systematic Approaches to Word Choice

The systematic approach, complete with its Red Flags, helped us steer government writers away from another construction, which I have heard called "mountains of modifiers" or "noun sandwiches." Here's my favorite example: EPA has a program. The program awards grants for constructing plants that treat wastewater. The program is very large. (It's running to the tens of billions of dollars.) A friend of mine was writing a paper about that program. Finding an appropriate metaphor, she thought, she called it the "mammoth wastewater treatment plant construction grants program." I gave her a cartoon showing a wooly beast backed up to a fire hydrant . . . a MAMMOTH WASTEWATER treatment plant construction grants program.

I would have had no problem parsing her sevenfold noun sandwich if we had simply been talking to each other. Unfortunately, though, the written sentence doesn't use breath marks or other means to indicate grouping within phrases so that the number of different meanings theoretically available for a sequence of nouns (technically, noun-adjectives and nouns) doubles for each layer of the noun sandwich. After commenting in our manual on the rhythm, or lack of it, of such phrases, we left our reader with a rule of thumb: expand noun sandwiches of three words the first time they appear; always expand four-word sandwiches. Expanding these phrases containing compound nouns (also called "complex nominals" in the literature) is hard in theory, because many meanings can lead to the same phrase. (Enter the mammoth.) But in an application—when a writer with a generally good ear knows the meaning of the phrase—the operation is simple. Would anyone have a problem with converting

Direct product design regulations

into

Direct regulations for the design of products

or

Direct regulations for designing products?

So why leave the reader guessing whether you were talking instead about
   Design regulations for direct products?
   After taking the time to define nominalizations (we chose "nouns with verbs inside them, like *prepar-ation*") we pointed out that they encompassed another set of constructions that are frequently criticized in style manuals. Haven't we all seen lists like this?

DO NOT SAY THIS	SAY THIS
give consideration to	consider
was in attendance at	attended
make provision for	provide for

The recommendation in all three examples is to do away with a nominalization in favor of the root verb. A systematic, Red Flag approach can give writers a chance to undo all inappropriate nominalizations.

Occasional instances of nominalization are not wrong, of course, or even inelegant. But nominalizations are pandemic in government prose. If we point them out one by one, we will fall into the trap I mentioned at the beginning of this article: we will point to isolated instances without finding the pattern behind them.

* * *

Most of my work in government has been to make better writers. This mostly means exhorting them to organize more to meet the conditions we work under: to get information across quickly and to differentiate it from the other masses of information their reader will be processing that day. I believe the devices we introduced in our manual help in letting writers streamline their own material by getting at recurring flaws in their writing in a systematic way. I don't believe in merely reciting the collection of anecdotes that they could see in most books on style.

I have not, however, trained government writers who write primarily for the public. At EPA, that staff is very small; most of the public writing comes from scientists or managers drafted for a particular job. In other words, the people who express the views of our agency were rarely trained as English majors. They're the ones that English courses should catch, though, because once they have been in government for a while, it's too late. The worst writers I have seen learned to write in the government, with the worst features of bureaucractic writing held up as de facto models.

Once you've been in government for a while, you learn its language. Its lingua franca isn't that of the general public; it's probably not even the most efficient way to communicate, even within the government. If we can catch government staff before they are fluent in the lingua, however, and teach them systematic ways to modify their writing, they'll stay better writers.

Bibliography

Adams, John R. "Abstract Nominalizations in General Sentences of English." Diss. University of Pennsylvania, 1976.

Bernstein, Theordore M. *Watch Your Language.* New York: Pocket Books, Inc., 1965.

Chomsky, Noam. *Syntactic Structures.* The Hague: Mouton & Co., 1957.

Harris, Zellig S. "Transformational Theory." *Langauge,* 41 (1965), 363-401.

Lees, R. B. *The Grammar of English Nominalizations.* 5th ed. 1968; rpt. Bloomington: Indiana University Press, 1960.

Levi, Judith N. *The Syntax and Semantics of Complex Nominals.* New York: Academic Press, 1978.

Mitchell, Richard. *Less Than Words Can Say.* Boston: Little, Brown and Company, 1979.

Newman, Edwin. *Strictly Speaking: Will America Be the Death of English?* New York: The Bobbs-Merrill Company, Inc., 1974.

12

Models for Writing

RICHARD C. NEWTON

Richard C. Newton did his undergraduate work at Southern Methodist University and his graduate work at the University of California at Berkeley, receiving the Ph.D. in 1971. His major field of academic study is the literature of the English Renaissance, with particular interest in prose and the evolution of prose style in the late sixteenth and early seventeenth centuries. His pedagogical interests in prose began with his first teaching position as a Woodrow Wilson Teaching Intern, at Bishop College in Dallas, Texas, during the years 1964-66. These interests continued and expanded; he has served as Writing Coordinator and Director of the remedial writing program at Temple University and as instructor of the first three required practica for graduate assistants teaching writing. He is currently chairman of the Temple English Department.

Probably the most "invisible" item of our social environment is, or has been until relatively recently, our language. This truism we recognize as the stuff of linguistics courses, where it's our delight to recognize what we daily experience and never notice, and to a certain extent of literature courses as well. In both sets of courses we habitually expose to scrutiny the operations of our daily language and what we believe to be its embedded ideologies. The process of making visible, of promoting to consciousness, what in the daily course of things our students do not notice is probably the most delightful thing about teaching. It's a fairly constant measure of success among teachers to observe how often their students gasp, or coolly allow, that they had "never realized that." Such habits of exposure, if they're good for our students, are presumably good for ourselves as well. We too should try to make visible, to promote to consciousness, what in the daily course of things we do not notice. For teachers of writing, this means subjecting to critical scrutiny our own assumptions about writing and the ideologies which may be embedded in those assumptions.

I would like to make a modest attempt at doing so in the following remarks. The question I'm going to discuss is that of "Which language?"

Which language do we teach? What is the model of acceptable, useful, and valuable writing that we as teachers hold in our heads?

Before taking up my subject, I want to let you know something about my interest in it, to let you know where—as we used to say—I'm coming from. I first became consciously or knowingly interested in the subject of models for writing in the same place where probably most college writing teachers developed whatever abiding interests in language we have—in graduate school. Having found my best and most stimulating teachers among those who were interested in the rhetorical effect of literature rather than normative models, I was in a very practical sense faced with the problem of what a "model" was. I knew what made literature interesting, but what made it good? I was especially shocked and challenged once by a declaration by one of my favorite teachers (tempered, to be sure, by the good spirits of a party) that he could no longer justify teaching John Donne as part of the academic literary canon over, say, a freshman essay. I felt certain that in any contest Donne would win, but my own training and experience informed me of the real problem of justifying that certain feeling. I hardly need to add that when I embarked upon my dissertation, my deeply felt but still somewhat detached professional concern about models for writing became a crisis. How could I write a big piece of prose, "real" prose? What should I sound like? What should my prose look like?

My second stimulus of interest in the problem of models for writing came from my first teaching experience. Between my MA and Ph.D. work, I taught at a small black college in the South. Educated myself in the white side of the segregated public schools of the same city as this college, I was totally unprepared for the absolutely stunning problems presented by what we have come to understand as Black English vernacular. This experience accelerated the reading in linguistics which an earlier interest in stylistics had already provoked, and it entailed a second crisis—a crisis of linguistic relativism. If the students are, in fact, doing nothing "wrong" with the language they use and with their styles of communication, who am I to intervene? Who am I to put them through hell trying to force them to change?

Both of these crises are perhaps familiar ones and have certainly had a fairly substantial currency in the academic community for the last couple of decades. The anguish of teachers who have been informed by the work of scholars like William A. Stewart, J. L. Dillard, and William Labov was in the late sixties and early seventies a common theme of discussions about writing, and a major component in the formulation of writing programs. That discussions of the legitimacy of teaching a "standard" dialect have cooled now does not, I believe, indicate that the crisis has been resolved—only that most teaching programs have acceded to what are perceived as unavoidable social demands. The crisis of the academic canon has found institutional legitimation in Black Studies, Women's Studies, and other special programs, while questions of models for writing, like questions of dialect, have tended to fade from view. Responsible writers of texts on writing, however, nowadays almost always give a nod to the legitimacy of nonstandard dialects, though easily affirming the necessity of mastering the "standard" dialect. Responsible authors will give some prominence to the question of stylistic models as well.

Exemplary for their reasonableness and forthrightness on the question of models for writing are John Halverson and Mason Colley, in their intelligent text, *Principles of Writing*.[1] In the section entitled "Which Language?" they identify their immediate concern as "one part of a nebulous linguistic area called 'standard English,'" which, though defying "precise definition," "refers approximately to the language written and spoken by most educated Americans and Englishmen." Having narrowed the territory thus far, they then further focus their concern on "a small but various segment, namely good written English." The examples of this are to be found among major literary figures of the nineteenth and twentieth centuries, "accomplished journalists," "critics," "historians," "scientists," and "public men," whose writings you will find in the major literary and public interest journals of the past hundred years or so. Examples to be *excluded* are "the sensational press, the learned journals, or the avant-garde literary magazines." Middle-brow writers are excluded, as is "the ponderous prose of a John Dewey, the crankiness of an Ezra Pound, or the 'oriental magnificence' of an F. R. Leavis." Halverson and Cooley thus attempt to define a model by example, to narrow down the range of their (and our) subject through inclusions and exclusions of exemplary writers; they attempt to define a *corpus*. This seems to me a minimal first step for any teacher. We have to know what to expect, what we are trying to elicit from our students. Identifying the exact features which unite all our writers in a common corpus, however, is an extremely difficult task, and I certainly won't try to accomplish that in this discussion. But I am going to look at some of its aspects and will try to elucidate some of our assumpions in teaching writing, in particular some assumptions about grammar and style, with the hope of suggesting some of the more important ideologies which seem embedded in those assumptions.

My main concern is with Halverson and Cooley's final remark on the question of Which Language: "this rhetoric is based on how good writers do *in fact* write English, not on how we might happen to think they *ought* to have written." Like a good contemporary grammar book, they aim to be descriptive, not prescriptive. This aim, however, is clearly belied by their setting up of the corpus in the first place. Even if we agreed with their exclusion of "bad" writing, we would have to insist that they had excluded some "good" writing as well from their model. Claiming that their work is merely descriptive, they clearly are engaged in "imperative" writing. *Principles of Writing*, like all rhetorics that I know of, describes how its authors think writing *ought* to be done. Though trying to deny that this is the case, its authors are at least honorably frank about the writers and kinds of publications from which they derive their imperatives.

Now, it seems to me that this ought to be obvious to anyone who teaches writing, indeed to anyone who teaches at all. Teaching means teaching a set of imperatives, and those imperatives have to come from somewhere. I believe that it is important, any time but especially now—as the teaching profession faces both financial and intellectual crises—that we try to become more aware of where those imperatives come from, and that concomitantly we become aware that they are not the only ones available. We need to understand the reasons for and implications of our choices, to consider what other choices we might make, and to take responsibility for the choices we finally do make.

As I have already told you, I have been rather seriously interested in this question of choices for some time, but I have been especially provoked to think about it by the recent book by E. D. Hirsch, Jr., *The Philosophy of Composition*.[2] Hirsch argues, just to the contrary of my position, that writing teachers do not, in any serious sense, have control over their subject. If anything, he argues, it's the subject which controls the teachers. The core of Hirsch's argument lies in his claim that there are, in the words of one of his chapter titles, "Progressive Tendencies in the History of Language and Prose" (Chapter 3). These "progressive" tendencies are towards "efficiency" or (in the case particularly of prose) "easy readability." Prose, Hirsch argues, has been, like language itself, slowly moving in the direction of ever more regular syntax. "Increased regularity of syntax," Hirsch states, "in itself makes language more efficient 'as an instrument of expression.' " And "This normalization of syntax alone makes modern prose a more functional instrument than the prose of the past" (p. 58). Prose is claimed to be naturally evolving toward easier "readability."

While admitting that it's impossible to make generalizations about the progressive simplification of syntax which show a consistent validity from writer to writer, Hirsch maintains that "in all the long-established grapholects, both the history of language and the history of prose progress towards greater regularity of syntax" (p. 57). But when he turns his attention to particular authors and texts, the interference of detail with this very large generalization becomes quite telling. Citing Jonas A. Barish's study of the prose style of Ben Jonson,[3] Hirsch accurately summarizes Barish's conclusions about the respective prose styles of Shakespeare and of Jonson: "Shakespeare's prose fulfills expectations and quickly resolves syntactic groups. Jonson's style deliberately baffles expectations . . . " (p. 68). Hirsch then proceeds beyond Barish, to describe Jonson as making "the communicative error of modeling written discourse on oral conversation." This claim is strictly Hirsch's. Barish, to the contrary, claims not that Jonson was imitating speech but rather that he was combining a variety of stylistic and linguistic models to serve multiple dramatic and philosophical ends. The difference is small but decisive. A writer indeed commits a "communicative error" if she's trying to communicate something and adopts the wrong model for doing it.

The point of Barish's analysis, however, is that Shakespeare and Jonson are engaged in communicating different information and so have appropriately adopted different models of communication. Shakespeare's plays (and Barish notes that it may be "excessively obvious to observe this") "constitute a dense network of cause and effect" (pp. 78, 79), hence the fulfillment of syntactic expectations and consistent closure which we find to be characteristic of his prose. "Jonson's world, by contrast," he notes, "is not causal, and character does not interact with character" (p. 79). More speculatively, but with equal point, Jonson's prose seems to reflect "a world so static that nothing in it is subject to change" or "a world so bewildering and disintegrating that nothing in it seems causally related to anything else" (p. 77). Hirsch reduces Barish's comparison of Shakespeare with Jonson to a simple dichotomy of "good" and "bad." Jonson is simply one of many sixteenth-century authors "whose instincts for prose happened to be less genial and *prefigurative*" than those of ... Shakespeare" (p. 69, my emphasis).

On the basis of his argument for "progressive tendencies," Hirsch can then claim that to teach composition is simply to teach the art of paraphrase: "in principle a revision of a prose passage *must* be able to convey the same meaning, if the teaching of composition is to have any point at all" (pp. 85-86). How essential this claim is to Hirsch's overall theme is apparent in his approach to Shakespeare and Jonson. By purging thematic meaning from what he regards as stylistic features, he can assume an equivalence of intent, roughly simple communication of fact (or "gist"), on the part of both authors and then say quite rightly that it would be in some relevant sense easier to get facts out of Shakepeare's prose than out of Jonson's. The importation of this doctrine of paraphrase into the pedagogy of composition serves the purpose of connecting the theory of "progressive tendencies" with an approach to teaching. Unlike that of Halverson and Colley, which takes responsibility for its models, this approach disclaims virtually all moral responsibilities and grants to the teacher the ethically pure role of merely cooperating with nature. "Nature" dictates the tendencies of prose. And the same "meaning" can be conveyed by one style as another. So we only need to know what "suits nature," and *that* is the direction in which we lead, or push, our students.

Hirsch's theory of composition is worth considering because it lays out a fundamental position for teaching. Most practically, it frees the teacher from charges of tyranny, either stylistic ("I *want* you to say it this way") or semantic ("*This* is what you should say"). That is, it frees the teacher from the anxiety of the two crises to which I refer above. Questions of style, including grammatical forms, are simply matters of nature and evolution, not the choice of the teacher at all. And there *are* no questions about content. The composition teacher (*qua* composition teacher) is not concerned with content at all, only with the translation of a meaning from a less readable form into a more readable one. This theory has its appeal. It frees the conscience of the teacher and allows us to coerce the recalcitrant student:

> . . . unless it were possible for a revised text to convey the same meaning as the original in a more readable way, we would not need to teach a student how to write readable prose. The student who protests that he *did* say what he meant would be right, and the teacher of composition could close up shop. (p. 87)

Armed with Hirsch's theory, the teacher need never face the possibility that that protesting student might be right. Hirsch gives us teaching without tyranny and without anxiety, teaching without ideology, teaching without meaning.

I believe that Hirsch's position is entirely incorrect, incorrect largely in its basic arguments, incorrect totally in its basic conclusion. To the question of what is involved in the choice of a model, Hirsch's answer is "nothing"; we are merely cooperating with Nature. Teaching composition is merely the teaching of readable paraphrase, not the teaching of meaning, significance, or value. I, to the contrary, argue that teaching composition, like all or at least most other teaching, is profoundly ideological and value-laden and that far from merely teaching students to "express themselves" more efficiently, we are teaching them as well, even teaching them mainly, what they should express, even who they should be. I say that ideological teaching is inevitable; it can't be avoided.

When we teach writing, as Hirsch points out in the first and best chapter in his book, we teach fictions:

> . . . one of the important functions served by scribal conventions is to characterize the implied author and the implied audience and, by this means, to define semantic shape and scope. . . . For, without an imlied author and audience, no degree of explicitness—including the highly elaborate explicitness of legal writing—could suffice to secure meaning. (p. 29)

When we teach students to write, we teach them conventional fictions. What is the mind of a good writer like? What is the mind of a good reader like? What do they expect of one another? How does a writer elicit those expectations and fulfill them? When we teach students to write, we teach them to "act like" good writers. Possibly, of course, we might succeed in teaching some students to perform this "act" *merely* as an act, a performance, a play. Such a task, however, is almost certainly beyond the scope of most teachers and most students. Most of our students are amateur writers, not professionals. In amateur theatrics, a director selects an actor largely because she fits the part, or rather the part fits her. Only of a professional actor do you expect that she fit herself to the part. The distinction between drawing out one's own personality and invoking acquired skills to create a persona is often a subtle one, but it's a crucial one with which any successful director of amateur theatrics is familiar. Now, with world enough and time, writing teachers might take a "professional" approach to their students. This is, in fact, generally the approach suggested by most rhetoric books even today. We could teach our students a set of skills and masteries which leave their basic attitudes and values unchanged. Both anecdote and research, however, indicate that this is not how most writers learn to write. Successful teachers instead invoke students' existing skills and attitudes and work from there, trying to get students to notice what they know and can do and then to do it more and "better." The "better," of course, is the catch, for we have to *convince* students to *want* that "better." That is, we have to change their minds. So at the end of the typical course of college writing instruction, of however many semesters, the student is still an amateur; her writing is still more or less uncontrolled self-expression and not the presentation of a self-distanced rhetorical artifact. But if the instruction itself has been successful, that writer's self will have been changed in significant ways. It will have been at least partially shaped into the self of a good writer. The unchanged writers, these are our failures.

Good writing, that is to say, requires the writer to assume the fictional self of the good writer. Though this self *is* a fiction, it is a fiction which most students of writing must come to believe is true, and to adopt as their own, if they are to make any progress as writers. The sources of this fiction, of course, lie in the texts which our culture or our profession values. They lie in models. All our teaching of writing, then, if it is coherent, presents these models, whether directly or indirectly. It is on the basis of the models that we correct students' writing and present directions for improvement. It is implicitly against these models that we measure students' progress.

Such models are of course not merely listings of features, though they do contain lists. For instance, there are some lexical items to be avoided; don't use *as far as* as a preposition, *like* as a conjunction, *them* as a plural demonstrative. And, of course, as part of what we call the grammar of language, there are alternative approved forms; use instead *with respect to* as the preposition, *as* as the conjunction, *those* as the plural demonstrative. Similarly, there are syntactical rules acceptable in many spoken dialects which are barred from good writing; don't write *try and, not no,* and so on. Many, if not all, of these lists and rules are occasioned by the fact that writing, not being a simple transcript of speech, is an artificial construct. It is not "natural." Being unnatural, it is decisively *shaped*. It assumes its forms on the basis of a set, if a very large set, of conscious and semiconscious decisions made either by the present executing writer or by writers in the present writer's past. Now I suppose that that is not very startling: "writing expresses consciousness." But to repeat, when we teach writing we are trying to get our students to subscribe to a conscious model, to make the writers of the past become part of *their* past. We are perhaps even trying to get our students to subscribe to a model of consciousness—to a model of how to interact verbally, but not only verbally, with the world.

Well, then. When we ask our students to write, we are asking them to learn, to believe in the wisdom of, to internalize, and to *use* a model (explicitly) of description and expression and (implicitly) of analysis and synthesis which has been shaped over literally hundreds of years by writers before them. The model is the result of a long tradition of writers' ideas about language, about written language, and about the relation of language to the nonverbal universe. In a technical sense, then, to subscribe to the model is to subscribe to an ideology, a structure of ideas. Again, we all know this. We all know that "style is meaning." How extremely we hold that idea no doubt varies with our individual critical positions, but I presume that all of us (except E. D. Hirsch) must believe it in some form or another.

I would like to discuss some of the ideological implications of our ideas about what good writing is at two levels: usage or "grammar" and sentence style.

At the level of grammar, a number of rules are consistently taught, indeed almost fetishized, which students find difficult to master but which are widely regarded as essential components of good writing. Notable among these are the rules concerning dangling modifiers and syntactic parallelism. The main reason we have to teach virtually all students the rules for avoiding the dangling modifier, I suspect, is that this particular "error" is made possible by a syntactic pattern that is relatively uncommon in speech, the introductory sentence modifier. I don't mean to say that such modifiers never occur in speech, but the phrasal sentence modifier (indeed, I think, the nonrestrictive modifier in general) is far more typical of writing than of speech. I would speculate, moreover, that most speech instances of sentence modifiers, and perhaps nonrestrictive modifiers in general, originate from scribal rather than oral sources. But in any case, a good deal of direct teaching and error-correction is devoted to teaching the avoidance of the dangling modifier.

Why do we war against the dangling modifier? In theory, of course, there's the problem of "readability." Dangling modifiers present problems of interpretation, or so at least most of us have on occasion been rash enough to claim, presenting howlers like this one as examples: "Standing on one leg in the swamp, Joe saw the blue heron." Some of the more intelligent writers on the matter, however, quite correctly do not resort to this usually false claim. W. Ross Winterowd, for instance, says that the problem is strictly a stylistic one, and not a matter of readability:

> The problem . . . is not really one of meaning, for any reader will know what is intended in the sentence [cited above]. The reason for avoiding dangling modifiers is that they say to the reader that you, the writer, are not in control . . . . Therefore, this error, like many others, diminishes the value of what you write.[4]

The same concession to good sense is made by Ebbitt and Ebbitt: "Dangling modifiers are to be avoided chiefly because educated readers do not expect to find them. As a rule there is no real question of the intended meaning of the sentence, and in context the dangling phrases are not apt to be conspicuously awkward or as nonsensical as they seem in isolation."[5] Ebbitt and Ebbitt do argue that a needless expenditure of energy may be required to decode the sense of a dangling modifier, but context almost always delivers the sense immediately, and often even context is not required, as in the stock-in-trade absurdity of the English teacher like the "blue heron" sentence quoted above. In fact, there must often be a greater expenditure of energy to see that there is a dangling modifier present at all than to decode the meaning of the sentence. A sentence like the following, for instance, the Ebbitts note "sometimes appears in edited prose": "Born in England in 1853, John MacDowell's seafaring activities began after he had migrated to this country." I think that there are many of us who would despair of *ever* convincing most of our students that there is some problem with this sentence. And there may be more than a few of us who ourselves would not be inclined to see anything wrong with it. Just where to draw the line is a problem, but in some cases the expenditure of energy required to detect the dangling modifier is simply too great, and we permit ourselves the indulgence of the "absolute phrase," as it is called by Frederick Crews:

> Some absolute phrases look precariously like dangling modifiers ... but we don't hear them that way.
> a. *Considering the demand,* the price ... is still ... low.
> b. *Generally speaking,* Melody's memory is smoky.[6]

As these last examples show, there is less than universal agreement about what a dangling modifier is.

Before we can detect a dangling modifier we have to learn an explicit grammatical rule which describes it. The rule we think we know may vary from person to person. And the character of the rule, in turn, will depend upon the theory of grammar to which we subscribe. First of all, at the descriptive level, some formulations of the rule are concerned only with the dangling participle, others with the dangling introductory phrase. Most of us are unlikely, I think, to remember which formulation we were first taught or which has made the strongest impression on us. But the way we formulate the rule will influence whether we see a dangling modifier in the following sentence: "With a little more time, I'm sure you wouldn't phrase the sentence this way."[7] Does your understanding of dangling modifiers regularly include prepositional phrases? If so, then "with a little more time" may be a dangling modifier for you. But then there is the question of what makes the modifier "dangle." Does your version of the rule say that the introductory participle or phrase must modify the immediately following noun or noun phrase, or does it say that the subject of the sentence must immediately follow the introductory participle or phrase and must be modified by it? If the former, then you may not have tended to regard the "John MacDowell" sentence as containing a dangling modifier. If the latter, then you have spotted a dangling modifier.

But besides the problem of description of the rule, we have the question of how we understand its terms. Usually, school grammars say that the introductory element must "modify" the elements that it precedes. Many of us, I suspect, in the sentence above would interpret the phrase "with a little more time" as adverbial. If we do so, it cannot then be a dangling modifier, since it cannot "incorrectly" modify the wrong noun or noun phrase; being adverbial, it cannot modify a noun phrase at all. Those of us committed to a generative model of grammar, however, will hold a somewhat different notion of modification. Instead of defining modifiers by category, we will regard modifying phrases as surface representations of deep structure sentences from which the subject (and sometimes the verb) has been deleted. This is generally my approach, so I will regard the phrase "with a little more time" as being, roughly, a surface representation of something like "if you had had a little more time," or so I intended it as I wrote it. Seen in this light, the introductory phrase is clearly a dangling modifier. The generative school grammarian will require that the highest-level immediately following noun phrase be identical with the deleted subject of the introductory phrase.[8] Those who see modification in terms of categorization rather than of generation will be likely to interpret the matter less rigorously. That is to say, what we actually "see" in a sentence is in part a function of our previous learning of descriptive rules and of our basic commitments to theories of grammar. Moreover, such theoretical commitments range far beyond "mere" grammatical concerns, as the controversy between Noam Chomsky and B. F. Skinner in the 1960s so dramatically demonstrated.[9] Even when we are doing something so elemental as indoctrinating students about the dangling modifier, we are implicitly teaching, besides a descriptive rule, an implicit theory of grammar, and beyond that a philosophy of language and even of mind.

But what is the rule's function? Why do we enforce it? Part of the reason for the rule's existence, I think, derives from the exigencies of teaching. That is, the rule is in part an artifact of the pedagogical process. After all, even though in most cases the dangling modifier is no hindrance to reading, there *are* cases in which it can confuse and needlessly complicate the reading process. And in such cases, the needed correction is clear; see to it that the highest-level immediately following noun phrase is identical with the deleted subject of the phrase. Discerning just when the confusion truly exists, however, requires a good deal of tact and experience. How much simpler, then, just to teach the universal rule. It works every time. It gives a standard of judgment. It eliminates all possibility of ambiguity. It provides a rational standard. Or rather it provides a *technical* standard.

Students may often feel, in the "grammar" parts of writing classes, that they are getting bogged down in "technicalities." Their feeling is correct. The major thrust of our formulations of rules is toward technical rationalization, the reduction of the decision process to repeatable routine. We know, of course, that we first began seriously to study "the rules" as the middle class sought to equip itself with the emblems and symbols of the great, including the great's "conversation."[10] The rules became, in effect, a kind of shortcut to culture. The emphasis, however, tends to fall less on culture than on shortcut, less on "conversation" in its extended sense of verbal and behavioral style of life and more on merely imitable rule. The supposedly imitated "conversation" has of course long since disappeared. And what are left are now only the rationalizations of that conversation, the rules, and the processes—the techniques of rule formation. The products of this process are now the objects of imitation by, among others, the class whose conversation they were originally supposed to imitate. Though originally the behavior of a class, what is imitated by all writers now is the process of rationalization, a process seemingly with a life of its own. We see this independence in the war against the dangling modifier as well in many other grammatical concerns.

The insistence upon grammatical parallelism is another case in point. When a student writes, "It was witty, adventurous, thoughtful, and has a great plot, subplot, and characters," the red pencil will lash out. Happily, in this case the student has also switched tenses, so the moral that variation of structure in a series is "wrong" might perhaps seem reasonable. This next sentence, too, has two errors: "Grace likes to go to the movies, bowling, shopping, and especially likes to go on vacations." Now in both of these cases, it doesn't seem that readability is the issue. To the extent that the sentences are difficult to read, they are difficult because we *expect* items in a series to be parallel in structure. That is, if we find the immediate motive for parallelism in the quest for readability, it turns out that the rule which supposedly promotes readability must be in existence before lack of parallelism is permitted to be a problem. The rule, it seems, creates the problem. That the rule is the problem may not be entirely obvious in these students' examples, but consider the following, from *The New Republic*:

> Nature, of course, did not ordain the British to govern anyone else. But their rule has been humane, limited, orderly, and it has not diverted the natives with heady fantasies of authority from their destiny (alas everybody's destiny), which is to eke out a living.[11]

One may perhaps be too appalled by this complacent defense of colonialism to notice the error in parallelism (adj., adj., adj., *and* sentence). Actually, this "error" is ubiquitous in contemporary discourse, appearing in semiformal speech (like newscasts and so on) perhaps more frequently than the "correct" form and in print much more often than all but the eagle-eyed of us might realize. Its widespread and utterly unproblematic use goes unnoticed in school texts, which continue to insist on a quite rigid maintenance of identical grammatical forms in sequences. We require adherence to the rule, despite the currency of alternatives in both writing and speech and regardless of the general irrelevance of its application, most of the time, to readability. The habit of rationalizing usage into rule seems to triumph.

I think that this habit of rationalization in excess of need or of the facts of usage is clear enough. Its consequences are rather disturbing. The reasons given by Ebbitt and by Winterowd for avoiding the dangling modifier are, as far as they go, surely correct. We do avoid the dangling modifier because there's a rule against it; breaking the rule "looks bad." It suggests to our readers that we are intellectual slovens. That dangling modifiers, inaccurate parallelism, and so on are the marks of intellectual laxity is one of the major fictions of which we must convince our students if we are to get them to become good writers. But the impression of laxity or slovenliness is primarily a result of the rule's existence in the first place. It would thus appear that following any particular rule has no justification other than that of *politeness*, of manners. Manners are, of course, part of our social glue, and to some may be defensible as such. But I feel a little uncomfortable stopping there with the defense of difficult and restrictive rules. I am left feeling a little "naked." I either want to be able to defend a particular rule, a particular facet of manners; or I want to be able to defend the structure of manners as a whole, of which the rule is a part. Since I can't defend most particular rules as somehow triumphantly logical and self-justifying, I am led to consider generally the implications of grammatical manners as a whole.

The realization that the rules of Standard Written English are open to question, that they are not self-evidently better than equivalent rules in spoken dialects, is of course the cause of the linguistic crisis to which I referred at the beginning of this discussion: the call for a reevaluation of our intents in teaching Standard Written English at all. The challenge to our enterprise of teaching Standard Written English is articulated by William Labov, in his popular pamphlet *The Study of Nonstandard English*.[12]

> There is no reason to presuppose a deep semantic or logical difference between nonstandard dialects and . . . an elaborated style. Some aspects of the speech of middle class speakers may very well have value for the acquisition of knowledge and verbal problem solving. But before we train working class speakers to copy middle class speech patterns wholesale, it is worth asking just which aspects of this style are functional for learning and which are matters of prestige and fashion.

Though addressed in terms of speech, the challenge applies equally to the problem of writing. Is it really "worth it" to make students spend perhaps years of achieving mastery of the conventions of introductory modifiers and items in a series? And does such mastery have any functional value? Or is it, as Labov suggests, merely the marker of class membership?

Undeniably, the question of class cannot be purged from our considerations. Though it can no longer be seriously claimed that there is an upper class whose usage determines the content of schooling, it is certainly the case that the educated, who are predominately the controllers of capital, do acquire their habits of written verbal usage in school, habits which are in turn at least partially reproduced in their speech and are largely reproduced, on the authority of their being the usage of the educated, in the schools. The schools may be understood to produce and reproduce the markers of class. Against these markers, these school-based skills, there are such things as "working class" linguistic skills:

> In the urban ghettos, we find a number of speech events which demand great ingenuity, originality, and practice, such as the system of ritual insults known variously as *sounding, signifying, the dozens,* etc; the display of occult knowledge sometimes known as rifting; the delivery, with subtle changes, of a large repertoire of oral epic poems known as *toasts* or *jokes;* and many other forms of verbal expertise quite unknown to teachers and middle class society in general.[13]

Labov would like to see the schools draw upon these speech events whenever possible, though he recognizes that they cannot be "transferred wholesale to the school situation." The difficulties of transfer, I believe, are formidable, in part simply because of class conflict between teacher and student and student and student, but also because of a conflict in the natures of the two sets of skills—"middle class" and "working class"—themselves.

Drawing upon the research of Basil Bernstein as well as upon his own researches, Labov notes that middle class speakers use "longer sentences, more subordinate clauses, and more learned vocabulary," whereas working class speakers use a relatively restricted vocabulary and syntactic repertoire and reduce the amount of linguistic redundancy. Middle class speakers take a less personal viewpoint than working class speakers"; in working class speech, "the unique meaning of the person would tend to be implicit." Finally, "middle class speakers interrupt their narratives much more often to give evaluative statements, often cast in an impersonal style"; working class speakers more often excel at the games and role-playing listed by Labov above. "Middle class speakers seem to excel in taking the viewpoint of the 'generalized other.' " These features of middle class speech are rather exactly matched by the major rhetorical conventions identified by Mina P. Shaughnessy as marking schooled writing. As middle class speakers often intersperse evaluative statements in their narratives, so schooled writers vary their discourse "between concrete and abstract statements, between cases and generalizations." And as middle class speakers use elaborated syntax and vocabulary and hold in mind the viewpoint of the other, so schooled writers explicitly mark "the logical and rhetorical relationships between sentences, paragraphs, and larger units of composition," which of course requires an elaborated syntax and vocabulary and is designed specifically to meet the expectations of an "other," the reader.[14] The key to these distinctions, as Labov notes specifically of Bernstein, is "greater or lesser *explicitness*—and . . . more or less attention to the monitoring of speech."

"Explicitness," it should be noted, must be defined by convention: there are rules to follow in order to *be* and to *be seen as* "explicit." Schooled writers must monitor their writing to be sure that it follows the rules of grammar. Both sets of rules are incarnated in that "generalized other" for whom we write. Taking the role of the "generalized other," then, becomes the primary skill of the schooled writer—exactly the heart of the fiction of the implied author we teach and require. The restricted code, Labov notes, "is the style commonly used among those who share a great deal of common experience." An elaborated code we reserve for situations in which "we presuppose the minimum amount of shared information and experience." This latter formulation needs some modification, as the elaborated code in fact presupposes an enormous amount of shared information and experience, but it is the information and the experience of school. What we learn at school, when we are indoctrinated with the requirements of school grammar, is precisely that continual self-monitoring which forces an awareness of the Other. We subject ourselves to the rationalizing requirements of grammar and write "as if" the Other cannot understand us unless we adhere to certain technical requirements. The experience is one of alienation and self-division. And yet it is effected by an intense socializing process, one which we share with all other schooled writers.

This is a lot to hang on the poor dangling modifier and parallelism rules. Still, I believe it's clear that the real role of conventions and rules in Standard Written English is to require and assure the continuous self-monitoring which is the mark and requirement of intellectual discourse. Following these rules creates the fiction that the writer is rational, alienated, and self-divided. School-rule-following language amounts to a continuing *allusion* to the canons of reason, accuracy, and disinterest that are supposed to characterize intellectual discourse in general. Few grammar rules are defensible simply for themselves, but together they exact the toll of moment-to-moment self-monitoring, on specific technically defined principles, for the sake of the Other. This is the role of "grammar."

Style, as we know, we have freer choice of, but we still govern our choices of style on at least some principles. We *like* some styles better than others and gravitate toward them. And generally, as Hirsch says, we find some styles more "readable" than others. Readability, however, is not what makes us select them. If anything, we find them readable *because* we have selected them. In a passage I have cited above, Hirsch credits Shakespeare with "instincts for prose" which are more "genial and prefigurative" than those of most other sixteenth century authors. Well, it does happen that Shakespeare was writing just at the time that very serious discussion and experiments were taking place, out of which emerged, in large part, the general outlines of the mainstreams of modern prose. And Shakespeare, as Jonas A. Barish has shown (pp. 23-40), was strongly influenced by one of the major figures of the time, John Lyly. So Shakespeare's prose is indeed "prefigurative," since he, with many others among our literary forbears in prose, was in effect instructed in prose by Lyly. Lyly, of course, is infamous for having developed an obsessively mannered style, characterized by extreme and elaborate parallelism, parallel elements being of exactly the same length (isocolon), often matching element for element in syntax (parison) and in sound (paramoion). These stylistic devices are accompanied by a good deal of proverb lore and pseudo-science. Not all devices appear at one time, to be sure, especially in passages translated from other languages, but they appear with a persistency, nonetheless, that creates an almost seemless surface of obtrusive style, which most modern readers find unreadable but which most of Lyly's contemporaries seem to have found brilliant.

To show the nature of Lyly's influence on our style, I'd like to consider a representative and not particularly extreme passage, largely translated from Plutarch, on the nursing of infants.[15] The argument of the passage is that infants should be nursed by their mothers, not by wet nurses, "for is there any one more meet to bring up the infant, than she that bore it? or will any be so careful for it, as she that bred it?" That neat parallelism of the two concluding comparative clauses would please all teachers today, and few would find the alliteration of *bore* with *bred* too fussy. Most will find that the intimate connection between bearing and raising that is the point of the sentence is legitimately heightened by the alliteration. Moreover, the more distant alliteration of *bring up* makes the main alliteration even more powerful, as it brings out the pun in breed—both produce and educate—the inextricable linking of both senses being, again, the point of the sentence. This sort of stylistic intensification of, or even creation of, meaning goes on in Lyly so continuously that, as I have said, modern readers find him difficult. But it seems to have been the very density of the stylistic devices which pleased his contemporaries, teaching them what, with greater moderation, they could do themselves.

What Lyly constantly *does* is suggest an extremely orderly world, in which everything is connected to everything else: "for as the throbs and throws in childbirth wrought her pain, so the smiling countenance of the infant increaseth her pleasure." Pain is linked with pleasure; everything is linked by alliteration. It is the *linking* which is important. The implicit assertion is that the linking is natural. "Wheat thrown into a strange ground turneth to a contrary grain, the vine translated into another soil changeth his kind. A slip pulled from the stalk withereth, the young child as it were slipped from the paps of his mother either changeth his nature or altereth his disposition." Lyly presents it as a fact of nature that the mother should be the nurse. What appears to be a strictly logical, though stylistically enhanced, argument before becomes an argument in excess of logic, an argument of fable. In a context in which everything is linked to everything else stylistically, the proverbs assume the same kind of link, something between logic and analogy, but with the continuing appeal and semblance of inevitability and reason. In Lyly the content argues connection; the style implies it. It is from this style that Shakespeare developed the prose of his plays, with their "dense network of cause and effect," their deep hints of analogical relations, their profound sense of the connectedness of things.

The implications of the rationality and coherence of the world in Lyly's genial style have of course been considerably modified by subsequent developments. At the very time that Shakespeare was realizing in his plays the brilliance of expression and insight which Lyly only prefigured, a countermovement in thought and style was just beginning to burst forth. In style this movement, generally known as the "anti-Ciceronian" movement, opposed the figurative, syntactic, and phonological devices of stylists of Lyly's ilk, on the grounds that they made greater claims either about the nature of the universe or the personal authority of the speaker than were justified.[16] Among the number of these anti-Ciceronians was Ben Jonson, whose oppositional style E. D. Hirsch declares to be "bad," when in fact it is simply a style which declines to make the claims about the integrity and orderliness of the world and the personal understanding of the author that Lyly's does. Another exemplary "bad" style is that of another anti-Ciceronian, Robert Burton.

Burton seems to share somewhat Lyly's belief in the rational coherence of the world and hence the rational validity of metaphor and proverb. But far from supporting this belief with stylistic devices of parallel syntax and sound, Burton completely eschews both. He is a persistent breaker of parallelism, and never echoes Lyly's repetitions of sounds. His own rather different discussion of the nursing of infants can illustrate how an anti-Ciceronian modifies the Lylian and Shakespearean sense of the connectedness of things:

> A more evident example that the minds are altered by milk, cannot be given, than that of Dion, which relates to Caligula's cruelty; it could neither be imputed to father nor mother, but to his cruel nurse alone, that anointed her paps with blood still when he sucked, which made him such a murderer, & to express her cruelty to an hair . . . .[17]

Burton's unLylian and unreaderly syntax can be seen in this passage in the weak reference of *he* to the genitive *Dion*, the "incorrectly" placed *neither* (parallel neither to the first nor to the second prepositional phrase), the telling indefinite reference of *which* (to the predicate "anointed her paps . . ." or to *blood*), and the paralleling of noun phrase with infinitive phrase ("a murderer" with "to express"). The syntax offers little easy guidance to the reader, and there are no phonological devices to perhaps suggest some connection which the syntax fails to make. Burton's *expository* procedure is equally unhelpful. To be sure, he offers an apparently logical narrative cause for Caligula's cruelty. But in expressing his nurse's cruelty "to an hair," is Caligula behaving in his own way as was the nurse who perverted an innocent, that is, imitating her behavior? Or is he expressing the thirst for cruelty which he learned from the bloody pap itself? The same question arises with Tiberius, "who was a common drunkard, because his nurse was such a one." Did he get the fatal taste from his nurse's milk, or did he learn the fatal behavior through imitation?

The thesis of Burton's paragraph claims physical causation, "that the minds are altered by milk," but while the discourse seems to develop this proposition, the logic drifts to suggestions of imitation. Both options are kept open: "And if she be a fool or dolt, the child she nurseth will take after her, or otherwise be misaffected." It is finally only in the course of a discussion of another topic that Burton actually does make the clear statement which we have been missing so far: "For . . . passions corrupt the milk, and alter the temperature of the child, which now being moist & pliable clay, is easily seasoned and perverted." Such an assertion makes exactly the connection between the spiritual and the natural which is the point of Lyly's prose, but it makes it on the basis of a specific physico-psychological theory, not as part of an overall assumption of a coherent universe. It's a theory, moreover, which Burton holds uneasily, and he drifts in and out of a commitment to it as he drifts from one argument to another. He weakens the presentation of his commitment by avoiding a straightforward exposition of his argument as narrative and logic, and by avoiding at the same time, unlike Lyly, the use of stylistic devices which give a suggestively integrated and coherent texture to his discourse. As many critics have suggested, these particular features of Burton's style express a general anxiety of anti-Ciceronian writers about the nature of truth and a reluctance to claim an excessive personal authority.[18]

A concern like that of Burton and the anti-Ciceronians has been argued with a new relevance for modern style by Walker Gibson. "If we live in a pluralistic and fluxlike universe, what manner of word-man should we become in order to talk about it?" he asks. Asking indulgence for his assumption that only men write, I'd like to quote his answer:

> Well, we might at least expect a man who knows his limits, who admits the inevitably subjective character of his wisdom. We might expect a man who knows that he has no right in a final sense to consider himself any wiser than the next fellow, including the one he is talking to. The appropriate tone, therefore, might be informal, a little tense and self-conscious perhaps, but genial as between equals. With our modern relativisitic ideas about the impossibility of determining any "standard dialect" for expressing Truth in all its forms, we might expect the cautious writer to employ many dialects, to shift from formal to colloquial diction, to avoid the slightest hint of authoritarianism. The rhythm of his words will be an irregular, conversational rhythm—not

the symmetrical periods of formal Victorian prose. Short sentences alternating erratically with longer sentences. Occasional sentence fragments. In sum we might expect a style rather like *this*![19]

Like the anti-Ciceronians of the seventeenth century, Gibson proposes an essentially "humble" style whose principal marks are asymmetry and variation. He eschews marked formal features, especially parallelism and other large syntactic patterns. He encourages shifts of voice and tone. The point of his argument is specifically that we should not imply stylistically a greater authority than our knowledge of ourselves and of the world will permit. He does not quite say that there's no truth (though his capitalization of the word has the ring of irony), but he might well agree with Ben Jonson that "Truth lyes open to all; it is no mans *severall*." Gibson does not require that we anguish and writhe over our access to the truth, as Burton does, but he denies us the assurance of the Truth that Lyly seems to offer.

Good advice, I've always thought. But advice I've always found it hard to follow, both as a writer and as a teacher of writing. Mainly I find it difficult because Gibson is not describing the mainstream of English expository prose. The mainstream of English expository prose, I grant, even claim, is that valued and defended by E. D. Hirsch, the prose genially prefigured by Shakespeare, and before him by Lyly. It's a prose of rationalized connection between elements, the prose of parallelism and concord. It's also, of course, the prose of rationalized instruction. To whatever degree we may agree with Gibson about the desirability of a modern humble style, the exigencies of teaching, and the models of prose upon which that teaching is based, push toward another version of the writer. Some of the major features of this model I have already suggested. In the structures of grammar and usage, we promote an autonomous, alienated, self-monitoring rationalist. And in the features of style inherited from Lyly, I suggest, we promote an author committed to a belief in an integrated universe, who claims implicitly to understand it. To be sure, this autonomous and authoritarian persona is signficantly "softened" by doctrines such as Gibson's. We are not completely insensitive to the facts of the modern world. We do know Burton's anxiety, Gibson's diffidence. But Burton's prose is not "good" prose. And Gibson's is too quirky. In the teaching situation, generally, you must master something else, something prior, before you can write erratic and asymmetrical prose like Gibson's. You have to master the basics. "The basics," as we all know, are the basics of rationalized grammar and grammatically rationalized style, the style our language learned from writers like Lyly.

If we find our students expressing anxiety in the face of such a demand, we need hardly be surprised. They do not *feel* authoritative. They may say they believe in, but surely they do not in their daily lives experience, a cosmos of coherence. And if they live alienated lives, they are not self-monitoring—self-examining sometimes perhaps, but not self-monitoring. They do not experience a moment-to-moment judging of the self by specific rational principles. It is not an activity which our culture values and promotes. So, as I have said, we have to convince them that they should really want to be like that. We have to persuade them to want to become, as Richard Sennett has described them, "autonomous individuals."[20] Autonomy, according to Sennett, has two forms. The simple form is nothing more than "the possession of skills." Possession of skills, Sennett notes, echoing Daniel Bell, is like the possession of capital: "expertise is like the cash of the 19th Century entrepreneur in that whoever has it can be independent."

The argument that skill is cash will surely have occurred at least implicitly in an embarrassingly large number of our encounters with students. It gives you, we want to claim, at least some degree of "self-possession." Even better than cash, however, is *true* self-possession, the complex autonomy that is a matter not simply of skills but of character traits, those which lead to self-mastery. "Personal mastery is rare," Sennett writes; "it commands respect. But a self-possessed person does more than elicit respect. The one who appears master of himself has a strength which intimidates others." The autonomous individual is modeled by the successful bureaucrat. To be sure, we don't really mean to teach our students to intimidate others or to become bureaucrats. But we inevitably face the fact that we *are* teaching them, most of them, to enter some bureaucracy or other, to fill some niche in the chain of the world of paper and information processing which is the workplace of the educated. They will need the skills of the literate, we tell both them and ourselves, to do the work which they presumably are preparing to do. The point, of couse, is not that their bosses will hate them if their modifiers dangle (though some bosses educated "in the old days" in fact will), but that the rationalizing, alienated and self-monitoring mind which their avoidance implies is the appropriate mind for a bureaucracy. And if one is to work in a bureaucracy, why not become successful? Why not develop the mind beyond the prose in fact? Why not become truly detached, alienated, rationalized? Why not become *self*-controlled in the truest sense? Well, now surely when we try to promote in our students a commitment to the technical rationality of grammatical rules and to the model of coherence implicit in the conventions of discourse which we adopt for the sake of the Other, surely when we do this it is not our aim to produce generations of Sennett's autonomous individuals.

This extreme of self-rationalization that Sennett portrays as the autonomous individual is one which through assigned readings and daily homily we fight against. It's not for us, we're sure, and not for our students. We just want to *empower* our students, with the requisite writing skills to be sure, but also with the skills for good and effective living. We want to enfranchise our students as individuals. We need at least to consider, however, the possibility that the models invoked in this process of enfranchisement may contradict our more humane aims, that reading Thoreau, for instance, may clash with teaching parallelism and the authoritative thesis. The model of style upon which we base our writing may in fact be a useful instrument for the work of the world that most of our students will have to do. But we also want to believe that it is more than an instrument of learning. We want to believe that it *is* learning, the heart of the liberal education. But we need, I believe, to examine that notion.

Let's say that we are at least correct in our estimation of the usefulness of the model, that the model does nurture the verbal skills necessary for the world's work and for Sennett's simple autonomy. I believe we can agree that today there is some evidence that students, and their other teachers, may be coming to believe that this is the case. The return of a commitment of colleges to writing courses and particularly the growth of specialized ones like writing for business and technology would suggest a growing belief that we writing teachers may know what we're doing and that our work is worth its cost. Some of us, I know, may feel some discomfort with such courses because they strip out too thin a version of the model, because they focus too exclusively on the skills of simple autonomy and slight the development of the character traits of complex autonomy. Still, we do what we can with the "basic" course, and we're glad to see the public and economic reaction to what we have long claimed as the value of our work.

It is, after all, on the basis of an economic claim, implicitly in the past and more explicitly now, that we persuade students to adopt our models for composition in the first place. We may not all stoop to an economic hustle, but we cannot deny it as a factor in any renewed surge of student motivation we may perhaps detect in our classrooms. And if I am at all correct about the model, we are correct to do so. Or we would be if the very economic conditions which have led to this renewed interest in composition did not create a serious counterforce to it. What has provoked renewed interest among our students in acquiring skills, including writing skills, for jobs is the current condition of job scarcity. It's unfortunately true, therefore, that a large part of our hope for greater success in teaching the skills and developing the character traits we offer to teach and develop lies in enmeshing our students more and more deeply in competition for fewer and fewer jobs, jobs which elicit from them or require of them the attitudes and capacities we believe we are trying to instill. There are fewer jobs in two senses. There is literally less work for human beings to do. This condition of scarcity may pass, to be sure, though it isn't obvious to all that it will. But even if it does, there are nevertheless fewer and fewer jobs available which call on the full range of skills and character traits of the autonomous individual. The current dramatic process of the "proletarianization of white collar employment"[21] leaves less and less scope for the kinds of mental and expressive abilities which it is the aim of writing teachers to inculcate. Simply, fewer and fewer bureaucratic jobs call for the character traits of the fully autonomous individual; more and more call instead for a relatively narrow range of skills. The process concentrates power in the hands of relatively few managers, thus reducing the number of jobs "worth having," and increasing the pressures which those jobs entail. The abilities of the liberally educated have of course always been given lip service by business, at least at the level of discourse of such a magazine as, say, *Forbes*. And now we are hearing more than lip-service complaints from executives disenchanted with their office-full of MBA's. On such complaints we may hang our hopes for a revival of energy devoted to the study of what we have to teach. But to do so is a desperate move on our parts. It inserts students into an intensely competitive fray—there just aren't that many executive positions available—and dooms the great majority to frustration and depression. How long can we hold up the pretense of executive placement? How many of our students can even half-seriously believe in it? And for how long? This is the crisis into which our commitment to our models and the movement of the economy have led us.

There seems to me no immediate release from this bind. Education premised on preparing students to fill economically defined positions *which use what we want to teach* will in the foreseeable future be a depressed education, or so at least economic considerations would indicate. If these considerations are correct, it's hard to see how most of us can in good conscience go on teaching. The model upon which we base our teaching is irrelevant to most of our students' economic needs. If they reject it, we and they fail. If they accept it, *we* may succeed, but they will still be entrapped in failure. And to the extent that the awareness of this situation infiltrates our teaching, both teaching and learning will surely, *do* certainly, decay into mere formalities. We teach students to write essays which suit our model of "real" essays; they, perhaps even eagerly, learn to imitate a "real" business letter. But the model of the empowered self upon which we base our teaching is belied by the prospective economic situation of the great majority of our students. No one will *want* them to make significant and authoritative generalizations about their observations and thoughts; no one will *want* them to elaborate those generalizations into specific discourses, proposals, or refutations. No one will want them to think.

Now it seems to me that at this point there are two pretty clear choices we can make, if we intend to go on teaching. They may not be mutually exclusive, but I will treat them for the moment as if they were. We may adhere to our current model of individual authority and mastery, but we will find and try to inculcate new motives for pursuing it. In discovering, or inventing, new motives, we must be careful not simply to fall back on the best of our old motives—the motives of a liberal education—for those motives had an economic underpinning which no longer obtains. Most of our students will *be* the slaves who function at the pleasure of the "free" minority. The rhetoric of individual enfranchisement is so appealing that only with difficulty do I restrain myself from a paean to its values as my conclusion. But its blatant discordance with the current and future economic world restrains my enthusiam. A model of the enfranchised individual can only be maintained *in spite of* the economic model. That is, it can only be maintained as an oppositional or revolutionary position. The *reason* for enfranchising oneself, for declaring the independence of the self from the values and modes of expression of the community (of "the street") and for empowering oneself as a self-monitoring, alienated, autonomous individual—the reason for doing this is to oppose, resist, or seek to destroy the system which tells you that it does not need your precious and arduously acquired abilities. Resistance or revolution, of course, may be expressed simply as divorce (Coriolanus: I banish you!) or as discrete withdrawal (Candide: "Il faut cultiver notre jardin"). This latter, I suspect, is the course being followed by many intellectuals in and out of the academy as they find, for one reason or another, that the best they have to offer is no longer desired or sought—their presence, yes, and their work, more and more of that—but less and less of what they have to offer of the best of themselves as enfranchised individuals.

Teachers are often justly accused of seeking simply to make their students models of themselves. And if I am right about intellectuals' adaptation to the current crisis and its depressing future, the accusation may once again be justified. We are teaching our students powers that are irrelevant to the world they will enter, powers which they *might* expend in a life of revolutionary opposition but which, if they follow our model, will be spent in the cultivation of gardens. Now, since I tend to distrust the model of teaching as self-replication, and since I would identify myself with the solution of Candide, I feel especially impelled to consider the alternative model, though I do so with the trepidation of inexperience and, as I have said, contrary inclination.

The second response to the crisis of the model of the enfranchised individual is to drop it altogether. Give it up, for it only institutionalizes social powerlessness. We put people in schools to keep them off the streets (it's cheaper than jail) and out of the labor market. And through teaching we give them abilities which at their very best empower a life of happy irrelevance or lonely opposition. The alternative, I quickly insist, is not an end to education—ignorance is not bliss—but the adoption of an aternative model, a socializing one.

Exactly what the model would look like, in terms of features, it's hard to say, hard even to imagine. Its teaching methods, however, are in the process of creation. The teacher will be "decentered" from the classroom. Students will write cooperatively rather than competitively. The concept of "plagiarism" will be modified. The object of the writing experience will be the production of a product which satisfies communal, not personal, interests. The style, of course, will not be an academically dictated one which makes claims of autonomy and authority. Personal authority and its claims will be devalued. The writing class will promote the socially useful values of the collective and will instill the values of communal bonding. Communal sports and modes of discourse will be introduced. Students may even "play the dozens," as Labov suggests. This will be hard. Such a model of teaching completely contradicts the model of education which society currently dictates. So a large part of the work of the class will have to be in sensitizing the class to the disjunction between the class and the society. The class will become an instrument of critical consciousness. Students then will have the experience of collective social analysis. A sense of social understanding rather than the experience of social powerlessness will be institutionalized.[22]

Again, though, just what the "new writing" might look like, and on what bases we might correct students' papers and say, "No, not that, *this,*" are still to be imagined. The differences from our current model might be slight. Indeed, it might well be that those very technicalities of grammar which I have discussed above, the shibboleths of parallelism and of modification, might still be there to perplex the minds of our students, *but not as shibboleths,* not as membership cards in the club of the Others. If it should prove that our technical, rationalizing approach to grammar can be harnessed to the service of critical thought, then the features may remain the same, but their meaning will change. Likewise for larger matters of style. Perhaps indeed Gibson and Burton before him will *not* do as models for our new generation of writers. For perhaps this generation will be able to make sufficient commitment to a model of analysis, a critical ideology, that the anguish of a Burton or the diffidence of a Gibson will be inappropriate. But the alternative will be not the self-assurance of the autonomous writer but the socialized conviction of a group. Projects are under way around the country to develop journals of socialized tasks and communal production. Perhaps from these, models will begin to present themselves to us. In any case, models will have to emerge from practice, from the decisions of actual writers. A model cannot be a prior construct. But its construction will be facilitated by an awareness on the part of teachers that their expectations, when unexamined, *are* the model in a very powerful sense. We must begin with the understanding that writing is never neutral; it is the expression of more than the writer. And when we teach that expression, we *create* writers. It is our obligation to engage in the sanguine task of attempting to understand the models of our creative energies, of our teaching strategies, to interrogate those models closely, and to choose again if new choice is the first choice of our consciences.

Notes

[1] *Principles of Writing* (New York: Macmillan, 1965), pp. 4-5.

[2] *The Philosophy of Composition* (Chicago: University of Chicago, 1977).

[3] *Ben Jonson and the Language of Prose Comedy* (Cambridge, MA: Harvard, 1960).

[4] *The Contemporary Writer* (New York: Harcourt Brace Jovanovich, 1975), p. 509.

[5] Wilma R. Ebbitt and David R. Ebbitt, *Index to English,* sixth ed. (Glenview, IL: Scott, Foresman, 1977).

[6] *The Random House Handbook* (New York: Random House, 1974), pp. 164, 197.

[7] A particularly unhelpful comment of mine on a student essay exam.

[8] A grammatical structure is at a "higher level" than any element that it may contain. The higher-level noun phrase *John MacDowell's seafaring activities* contains the lower-level noun phrase *John MacDowell.*

[9] The controversy between Skinner, the foremost exponent of behaviorism, and Chomsky, father of generative grammar and exponent of philosophical rationalism and theories of innate psychological structures, reached its climax in 1971 with the nearly simultaneous publication of *Beyond Freedom and Dignity* and *Problems of Knowledge and Freedom* respectively.

[10] See for instance the polite acknowledgments by John Dryden in the prefaces to *Marriage á la Mode* and *Aureng-Zebe* of his indebtedness to the "conversation" of his patrons for the models of his style.

[11] *The New Republic*, January 20, 1981, p. 42.

[12] *The Study of Nonstandard English* (Champaign, IL: NCTE, 1970), p. 38.

[13] Ibid.

[14] *Errors and Expectations: A Guide for the Teacher of Basic Writing* (New York: Oxford, 1977), p. 240.

[15] *Euphues, the Anatomy of Wit, The Complete Works of John Lyly* (Oxford: Clarendon Press, 1902), I, pp. 264-66.

[16] See Robert Adolph, *The Rise of Modern Prose Style* (Cambridge, MA: M.I.T., 1968), for a summary discussion of the major seventeenth-century arguments.

[17] *The Anatomy of Melancholy* (New York: Tudor, 1927), pp. 283-84.

[18] See for instance the excellent discussion by Stanley E. Fish, "Thou Thyself Art the Subject of My Discourse: Democritus Jr. to the Reader," *Self-Consuming Artifacts: The Experience of Seventeenth-Century Literature* (Berkeley and Los Angeles: University of California, 1972).

[19] "A Note on Style and the Limits of Language," *The Limits of Language*, ed. Walker Gibson (New York: Hill and Wang, 1962).

[20] *Authority* (New York: Alfred A. Knopf, 1980), pp. 84-85.

[21] Henry M. Levin, "Back to Basics and the Economy," *Radical Teacher* 20, p. 9. Levin's essay provides a good brief overview of the relation of schooling to economics.

[22] See the similar approach to therapy by Richard Lichtman, "Therapy and Its Discontents," *Socialist Review* 61 (Vol. 12, No. 2) March-April 1982, pp. 91-106, and the extended discussion by Ira Shor, *Critical Teaching in Everyday Life* (Boston: South End Press, 1980).